The Work of His Hands

Targeting Your
Spiritual Gifts

Linda C. Triska

ISBN 978-1-0980-2591-5 (paperback)
ISBN 978-1-0980-2592-2 (digital)

Christian Faith Publishing, Inc.
832 Park Avenue
Meadville, PA 16335
www.christianfaithpublishing.com

Printed in the United States of America

Image Processing: Ryan M. Brewer, Digital Artist

Artwork Design: Kléte, LLC

Dedicated to my parents,

SAMUEL AND MARY FRENO,

who raised me in the admonition of the Lord.

Ephesians 6:4

BOOK REVIEWS

The book *The Work of His Hands: Targeting Your Spiritual Gifts* is a must read for those who truly want to know God in an intimate way. It's timing in my life, after close to forty years in ministry, was at a right-on-time moment. If you are searching for answers concerning the Holy Spirit and His spiritual gifts, this is the book for you!

Bishop Keith Conard
Faith Evangelical Center, Leavenworth, KS—Senior Pastor
Anchor Bay Evangelical Association—President

The Work of His Hands: Targeting Your Spiritual Gifts is eloquently written and masterfully tells the journey of how God puts his super on our natural.

This book is a practical guide to learn, grow, and exercise our walk in the gifts of His Holy Spirit in the human story. Not only will it inspire you with the ways in which God uses His people, but it also provides a challenging roadmap and tools to take your own journey in discovering the ways in which God wants to use your life.

A tremendous resource in taking a very complex topic and breaking it down to a very applicable level, *The Work of His Hands: Targeting Your Spiritual Gifts* not only shows how the Holy Spirit will use ordinary people but provides direction for you personally to step out in faith in the realms He will awaken within you.

Tom Hammel
Executive Administrator for SoCal Network
Assemblies of God

As I've read through *The Work of His Hands: Targeting Your Spiritual Gifts,* Linda Triska's well-written and very interesting story, I realized over and over again the power of a testimony. I can only imagine how the strength of this work will continue for decades. Generations will read and be moved by its content. The truth is, one will realize the possibility that they too have all the gifts available for their own lives.

The additional short stories included toward the end of the book will also bless you. I know the Lord will use this book to activate lives both now and for generations to come.

Linda's life journey is one to be admired exemplifying a life of strength, hope, and love. Enjoy and glean as Holy Spirit leads you to new possibilities for your life from this book and from its workbook as well.

Nellie LaBouef
Aglow International—Area President &
Southwest Coastal Region Generations Director
Author, *Intimacy Today—His Heart, My Heart*

This book, *The Work of His Hands, Targeting Your Spiritual Gifts,* is a wonderful tapestry of God's promised breakthrough and the power of our testimony. Along with connecting with and journeying through Linda's personal story, you will also gain unusual insight and revelatory impartation to gain the promises of God in your life today! This is truly a life's work, filled with stories and truths that will not only challenge you but will convict you to gain greater growth and forge a closer relationship with God and with His Holy Spirit.

Th.D Pastor Ben Lim
Ben Lim Ministries
His Way Life Church—Los Angeles, CA

In *The Work of His Hands: Targeting Your Spiritual Gifts,* Linda Triska dives deep into the supernatural and inspires readers to hunger for more of the Lord and more for His empowerment needed for the times we live in. You will be inspired by Linda's personal story of encountering the Lord and being overcome by His Spirit, and you will be given keys on the gifts of the Holy Spirit which will help target your own spiritual gifts. You will also read incredible stories of visitations of the Lord Jesus and His holy angels. In the day and age which we are living, many are longing for more than mere information. Many are longing for a true encounter with God and His Kingdom in the power of the Holy Ghost.

As you read this new exciting book, you will walk away with both the desire and the faith to step into a new dimension of the supernatural for yourself and your ministry.

Stephen Powell
Evangelist
Lion of Light Ministries—Pineville, NC

CONTENTS

ACKNOWLEDGEMENTS

First and foremost, I want to thank my Lord and Savior, Jesus Christ, for calling me to write this book. Without Him, there would have been no story to tell.

Special thanks to Kameron Surra. I don't know what I would have done without you!

My great appreciation to my husband, Brad, for urging me on to keep writing and for supporting me through this journey. God bless you for giving up many hours of our together time for the sake of this work.

Thank you to my daughter, Tawny, and her husband, Hunter, for the joy and enrichment you bring to my life.

A sincere thank you to my readers: Christine Darwazeh, Paula Foster, Dorene Marino, Tawny Pollard, and Pam Whitfield. Your heartening comments cheered me on to the finish line.

Many thanks and blessings to Pastor JJ (Jerry) Borja and Pastor Chris Montes for the hard work you both put in to design the website. You're the best!

My thanks to all of those who contributed to this book by allowing me to share your stories. They are an inspiration to us all.

Thank you to Ryan Brewer for assistance with the photographs. Your help came just in time!

My heartfelt thanks to Mary DeSantis. Thank you for sharing your invaluable insights, your expansive knowledge, and taking this adventure.

To God be the glory; great things He hath done!

PREFACE

Every once in a while, I run across a book that I can relate to and wholeheartedly recommend. *The Work of His Hands: Targeting Your Spiritual Gifts* is one of those books.

Linda's life story growing up in a little "nowhere town in Pennsylvania" struck me hard having spent my own childhood on an obscure island in Indonesia. Yet God's hand was upon her leading and guiding her long before she realized what He was doing and before she was able to connect the dots.

It was during the Voice of Healing years that she saw first-hand the healing miracles of Kathryn Kuhlman, A. A. Allen, Oral Roberts and the like and that exposure was drawing her towards her own destiny of a healing ministry. Even as a child, she would play "Oral Roberts" pretending to heal the sick as they were "slain in the spirit."

This book will excite all who read it as we all have a calling and destiny on our lives to fulfill. It was mapped out long before we were born. Psalm 139:16 tells us that we each have a book in heaven written with our days laid out by the Master Planner.

Parents will also be encouraged as they read how God works in children's lives. Never give up praying for them! We never know what the Lord will use to catapult our children into their own destiny.

Not only does Linda share her own life journey, but then goes on in Section 2 to teach on the spiritual gifts that the Holy Spirit equips each one of us with so that we can accomplish our God-given purpose. There is also an accompanying workbook to help identity those gifts.

Whether you are struggling to define your place in God's plan or are already on the road to accomplishing what He has called you to do, I highly recommend this book to you. Not only will it bless you in many ways but will move you closer towards God's blueprint for your life.

Mel Tari, Evangelist
Author, *Like a Mighty Wind*

INTRODUCTION

And it shall come to pass afterward,
That I will pour out my spirit upon all flesh;
And your sons and daughters shall prophesy,
Your old men shall dream dreams,
Your young men shall see visions
And upon the servants and upon the handmaids
In those days will I pour out my spirit.

—Joel 2:28–29 (KJV)

The visions would come at night when only the chimes of the living room clock and the rhythmic breathing of my sleeping husband lying beside me could be heard.

On this particular cold, February morning, I struggled out of a sound sleep at 3:30 a.m., trying to gain some sense of consciousness. For seven nights, I had been having a series of spiritual visions, and I knew the Lord was awakening me again to join Him in that secret place that only He and I could share. The Lord Jesus would visit me, and we would enjoy fellowship together. There were times when He would teach me truths; other times, He would give revelation. And sometimes we would travel in silence, yet I was always keenly aware of His presence. We traveled in an "otherly" dimension, crossing various terrains. Each symbolized a specific time in my spiritual walk, often playing out like an Indiana Jones adventure.

Just as Paul said in 2 Corinthians 12:2 when he had a vision of heaven, "I don't know if I was in my body or out of my body," I can echo the same, but it was all very real and very tangible.

I propped myself up on my pillows on this night, waiting in anticipation for a continuation of the same type of vision, but this time, what I saw was completely unexpected! With sleep-encrusted yet wide-open eyes, I observed out of my peripheral vision, a flat, rectangular object suspended in midair, floating toward me from the right side of the bed.

It was as if time stood still and the physical realm dropped out. Brightly lit, this unidentified flying object stopped at the foot of my bed at eye level, directly in front of me. I curiously peered at it and, to my wonderment, identified it as a book. I could see it all very clearly and made note of every intricate detail: the artwork, the title, and the most shocking of all, the author's name—it was mine!

Then I heard a voice. I can't say if I heard it with my physical ears or in my spirit, but I certainly recognized it. I had heard it many times before. It was the voice of my beloved Lord. "This," He said, "is the book you will write." It was a distinct mandate from God Almighty!

I stayed in His presence until the gray shadows of daybreak were broken up by the rays of the dawning sun, at which time I arose and sketched out what I had seen. My thoughts were that one day—someday—I would write this book. I tucked it way back in the filing cabinet of my mind, in a drawer labeled, "Someday," and went off to start the morning coffee.

But someday came sooner than I had imagined. A month after the vision, I attended a spiritual renewal conference. The guest speaker was Jill Austin. Jill had a heavy prophetic anointing, and I tried to attend her meetings whenever possible. Amazing things would happen in her services, and this one was no exception—not by a long shot!

As the anointing of the Holy Spirit descended on that meeting, Jill moved out into the congregation and began to prophesy to several individuals. I was on the end of an aisle, and she passed by me to give a prophetic word to a young man in the back row. As she was coming back down the aisle, she stopped behind me, laid her hand on my shoulder, and asked me to stand. My heart was wildly beating in my chest, and my mind was spinning. To my utter astonishment, she spoke a word of knowledge. "There's a book that God wants you to write, and you know about it." The only ones who knew about that book were God, me, and my immediate family with whom I had shared the vision. Jill didn't know me or my name let alone know about the book. Even more bewildering was the fact that she went on to say that God wanted me to start writing it *now*.

Not long afterward, my next confirmation came by way of a pastor on our church staff, Pastor Gwen Tackett. On a Sunday evening, following the service, she stopped me and said, "Linda, every time I look at you, I see you writing. Are you writing a book?" There was no getting away from God's call. He had made it absolutely clear.

And so the journey began, searching the mountain of personal journals which I have faithfully written over the previous thirty-five years, revisiting my instructional materials on spiritual gifts, and digging out some of my long-forgotten sermons. I believe the release of this book is now for "such a time as this" all set on God's timetable.

To help you navigate through this book, Section 1 is the testimony of this ordinary woman living an ordinary life, in an ordinary world, touched by the hand of an extraordinary God. It's the story of how He took me through winding paths and uncharted territory to bring me into my destiny and calling. My hope is that, as you read this, you too will hunger to have this same God touch your life, and you will begin your own personal journey to fulfill His purposes for you.

Section 2 is a teaching tool on the gifts of the Spirit (1 Corinthians 12, Ephesians 4, and Romans 12) to help you target your spiritual gifts and "equip you with everything good for doing his will." It is the compilation of lessons that I have been imparting for many years in churches, conferences, and retreats.

In Section 3, I share some remarkable stories of people whose lives have been changed by the work of His hands through supernatural interventions and miracles. I have diligently tried to verify the accounts presented. Some are supported by facts and documentation; others…well, I leave up to you. Personal encounters with Christ can be expressed in words but cannot be shared in experience; they are one-on-one. Therefore, some experiences can be substantiated while others will have to be taken by faith.

As this last spiritual era, the dispensation of grace, quickly draws to an end, my desire is to see other "ordinaries" like myself rise up and begin to move in their individual gifts and callings with signs and wonders following. Joel 2 tells us that there will be a revival in the last days unlike any other spiritual visitation that has exploded and ebbed over the canvas of history. This move of God will not be led by only an anointed few; uniquely, it will be an outpouring on "all flesh"—including men and women, old and young, and children—all prophesying, dreaming God-instigated dreams, and seeing beyond the veil. It is a call-to-arms to the Church to destroy the works of the enemy and to bring in as many as possible to the knowledge of Jesus Christ via the supernatural work of the Holy Spirit's power, operating through those who choose to be on the front lines right before Christ's return.

And so, I present to you *The Work of His Hands: Targeting Your Spiritual Gifts*, evidence of God's hands honing and shaping lives through trials, tribulations, defeats, victories, and experiences with Him, being led each day by His Holy Spirit. He continues to look for ordinary people to do extraordinary work for His Kingdom. My prayer is that you are one of those who will seek to have life-changing encounters with Him, crawling after Him in desperation for His presence, and finding yourself in the vortex of the tornado of His Spirit, doing all that He has called you to do. I can guarantee it will be a wild and exciting ride!

In His service,

Rev. Linda C. Triska

SECTION 1

Under Construction

Yet, O Lord, you are our Father. We are the clay, you
are the potter; we are all the work of your hand.

—Isaiah 64:8 (NIV)

CHAPTER 1

In the Beginning

Humble beginnings is probably the best way to describe my origins. I was born in Western Pennsylvania in the small, unassuming town of Canonsburg, snuggled in the northeastern end of Washington County.

When I was young, in order to raise its (and my) importance, I would loftily say, "Oh, you know, where Perry Como is from." At that time, of course, everyone would knowingly nod, giving the desired response of being highly impressed, as if his fame had anything whatever to do with me. But then the younger generation came along, and the question was, "Who is Perry Como?" I then switched to Bobby Vinton, another famous denizen of Canonsburg. That worked for a while, but eventually, I ran into the same problem of a generation who was clueless as to the renown of Bobby Vinton. At that point, I decided to just say it was about forty miles southwest of Pittsburgh and left it at that, allowing Canonsburg to sink into anonymity once again.

My grandparents on both sides of my family were Italian immigrants who arrived in the United States in the early 1900s through Ellis Island, New York. From New York, they migrated to Western Pennsylvania and settled around the Pittsburgh area.

It was all in God's plan for them to come to America, because somewhere along the line, someone shared the Gospel of Jesus Christ with them, and they all received Christ as their Lord and Savior. Both families then began to attend the Christian Church of North America (CCNA) in Canonsburg. The CCNA was established by

Italian-Americans in 1927 in Niagara Falls, New York, and was part of the United States Pentecostal movement occurring in the early twentieth century. Today, it is known as the International Fellowship of Christian Assemblies, an affiliate of the Assemblies of God.[1]

The church my grandparents founded.

Spiritual DNA

My maternal grandfather passed away before I was born. As a result, my grandmother, Philomena, lived with our family for many years. Of all the grandparents, I knew her best. She was the most colorful character of our lot.

Rick, my younger brother, dubbed her "Phil," and that's what stuck. It somehow rather suited her. She was short, only standing about four feet, ten inches tall, and always seemed old to me with her thin gray hair pulled back in a bun and her slow, unsteady gait on thin, spindly legs. But she was always jolly, and her great round

---

[1] International Fellowship of Assemblies, Wikipedia, en.wikipedia.org/wiki/International_Fellowship_of_Assemblies_International, (December 3, 2013)

belly would shake when she laughed, reminiscent of Old Saint Nick. When we would make reference to it, she would become very serious and answer that she wasn't fat but that her stomach was "a-swell-a" (interpretation: swollen). Of course, we all knew better—she liked her pasta!

Before Grandma Phil gave her life to Christ, she had that legendary Italian temper, but God knew what He was doing with her. When she opened her heart to Him, it was with a welcomed abandon, and that fiery temper became a fire for the Holy Spirit. With great passion, she became an all-out soul winner for Christ. She had a great faith that did not waver.

When my mom was in her teens, my grandparents established another Italian Christian Church of North America in Burgettstown, Pennsylvania. On Thursday afternoons, Grandma and a friend would go door to door in search of other Italians with whom they could share the Gospel and invite to their church. And every Sunday afternoon after service in Canonsburg, the family would go home, eat their spaghetti dinner (spaghetti was always Sunday fare), pile into the family automobile, and ramble to Burgettstown to hold services at the new church. My mom's brother, Louis Montecalvo, pastored that fledgling church for several years. When he moved on to pastor a church in Florida, my dad's brother-in-law, Vincent Salituro, pastored there for many years until they took another church in Arkansas. Today, that church, known as the Burgettstown Christian Assembly, still stands as a testament to my family's obedience to God and is a part of my heritage.

Mangia! Mangia!

My dad's parents lived a good distance away from us, so I didn't know them as well as Grandma Phil, but they were certainly just as godly. My Grandma Constance gladly and readily accepted the Gospel immediately when she heard it, although Grandpa John didn't get saved until many years later. My memories of them are that they were both always kind.

Grandma always wanted to feed us—a universal Italian trait. She'd say in her broken English, "Lind (she always left the "a" off my name for some reason, although she seemed to put an Italian "a" on everything else!), Mangia! Mangia! (Eat! Eat!)," while shoving food toward me, and Grandpa was always pushing Grandma to cook something to feed us—as if she wasn't already!

The Next Generation

My dad was a full-time pastor. Most of his churches were around western and central Pennsylvania. After he retired, he became a prison chaplain until six months before he passed away at the age of eighty-two.

My dad was in his teens when his family got saved, but he would have nothing to do with Christianity. He knew in his heart that if he gave his life to Christ, he would be called to preach, and that ran contrary to his own plans. He loved music and played clarinet and saxophone, and his goal was to be a musician in a band. It was the big band era, and week after week, he would jam with the dance bands at the local town parks. But my grandma was a real prayer warrior and never quit praying for her children—all ten of them. Finally, at age seventeen, Dad couldn't fight the wooing of the Holy Spirit any longer. He slipped into the bathroom, the only private place in the house, and asked Jesus to forgive his sins and come into his heart. As a bonus, he received the baptism of the Holy Spirit with the evidence of speaking in tongues while kneeling there at the toilet! And sure enough, at age nineteen, he began to preach and never turned back.

Mom's story wasn't quite as dramatic. Whereas Dad was more on the serious side, Mom was always fun-loving and the life of the party. She loved to entertain people and make them laugh. Her best gig was to imitate others as if in a stand-up comedy act. It was an honor to be "mimicked by Mary." It was all in good fun, and everyone loved her.

Even in her hardest times, Mom had a positive outlook. Her favorite saying was, "This too shall pass," and she lived by that, her trust always being in the Lord. She was a lot like her mother in that way.

At eighteen years old, Mom decided that it was time to give her heart to Christ, and that's what she did. It was that simple. She was never about pomp and ceremony. She had a simple, easygoing outlook on life.

My parents met at that little Christian Church of North America in Canonsburg where both families attended and were married there in 1945, thus beginning a lifelong love affair until Dad passed into glory in 2006. Mom followed in 2012.

In retrospect, I can see that God's hand mapped out my family's destiny by leading my grandparents away from their familiar homeland of Italy to landing on the unknown shores of America. God had a plan to intersect their lives and bring them to a saving knowledge of Jesus Christ in the new land.

That truth has been passed down through our family generational line ever since. I too, like Timothy in the New Testament, have a rich heritage in God. As Paul wrote, "I have been reminded of your sincere faith, which first lived in your grandmother Lois and in your mother Eunice and, I am persuaded, now lives in you also" (2 Timothy 1:5, NIV).

But perhaps you are reading this and don't have the same spiritual heritage. The most important thing is for you to know Jesus yourself. If you have not made Him your Lord and Savior, you can be born again this very minute by saying this prayer:

> Jesus, I believe that you are the Son of God and that you died on the cross for me and rose again. I invite you into my heart and give my life to you. Please forgive me for all my sins and wrongdoings and grant me eternal life in Heaven. In Your holy name I pray, Amen.

If you sincerely meant that prayer, then your name is now written in God's Book of Life, and you are "born again" through the shed blood of Jesus Christ to live eternally with Him in Heaven. You never have to fear death because your place in Heaven is secure. And you will always have a Friend who will never leave you nor forsake you.

Now you have begun the great heritage of salvation through Jesus Christ to be passed down to your posterity. He promises that "if we confess our sins, He's faithful and just to forgive us our sins and cleanse us from all unrighteousness" (1 John 1:9, KJV).

And you have now stepped onto the path toward the destiny that God has specially designed for you. Begin to read the Bible with an open heart and mind. Pray every day, and attend a church where the truth is taught. These will help you grow in your faith.

I would love to hear from you if you have just prayed that prayer. You can send an email to me at the address provided in the back of this book. Congratulations! It's the best decision you have ever made. It's eternal!

CHAPTER 2

Shaping Influences

"Have you been waiting for me?"

Carnegie Hall in Pittsburgh, Pennsylvania, was filled with thunderous applause as Kathryn Kuhlman glided across the stage in her impeccable white flowing dress and red hair flying behind her. She had an undeniable presence and a dramatic flair that drew people to immediate rapt attention.

It was Friday afternoon. My parents attended Miss Kuhlman's services every week and, on occasion, with my two brothers, Ken and Rick, and me in tow. We would arrive long before the doors opened to get ahead of the droves of people lined up on the street in order to get seats down on the main floor. Dad and Mom were hungry for the move of the Holy Spirit, and they didn't want to miss a thing.

The song service would begin, and anticipation would rise as the glory of the Lord permeated the atmosphere. Miss Kuhlman would share a little from the Word, and then the healings would begin to take place. The gift of the word of knowledge and the gifts of healing would manifest as she called out maladies of every sort.

"Arthritis in the knees is being healed to my left. Stand up and walk in the name of Jesus. Over here on my right, a tumor is disappearing. Who is that? Come up here and share what God has done. Up in the balcony, someone is being healed of kidney disease. Where are you?" And so it would continue throughout the rest of the service, often for hours.

As a young child, I would mostly sleep through the services, but there were times when I was very much awake, fascinated by

27

the work of the Holy Spirit, watching as one person after another shouted for joy. They were instantly healed!

***

In my five-year-old eyes, he was an imposing man, though not necessarily tall in stature. In the 1950s, A. A. Allen's huge circus-like tent dominated the Voice of Healing Revival scene. When he set up in the Pittsburgh area, Mom and Dad and we kids were at his meetings every night.

But more exciting than that was when A. A. came to our house for dinner during that crusade. There was a great deal of flurry in our humble duplex home preparing for his arrival. Mom arrayed me in my best yellow Sunday dress with a fluffy crinoline slip underneath and curled my otherwise straight blond hair. Brother Allen was gracious and unpretentious, but it was the amazing stories of the miraculous and outrageous manifestations of God's presence in his services that he shared around our table that grabbed my attention. I sat next to him the entire time he was with us, wide-eyed and enthralled. Again, God's supernatural power had captured my heart.

***

The smell of canvas and sawdust welcomed us as we trudged through the parking lot toward the Oral Roberts tent crusade. Even at six years old, I didn't mind sitting through his long-into-the-night services. Who could sleep anyway when healings and miracles were about to take place?

Dad was on the platform, so our family was able to sit in the "good" folding chairs down near the front. But it didn't matter how hard and uncomfortable those wooden seats were, I was able to witness firsthand the undeniable, miraculous hand of God.

The amazing healing that I remember most clearly was a young boy about my age who was crippled with polio, getting up out of his wheelchair, taking off his leg braces after Brother Oral prayed for him, and running across the platform unaided. The congregation exploded with praise!

Now Oral Roberts had a unique style when praying for the sick. He would sit on a chair as people with every kind of illness imaginable paraded up the side ramp and onto the platform. Then he would place his hand on each person's head and say, "Heal," and more times than not, they would fall down under the power of God (also known as being slain in the Spirit) and would stand back on their feet whole and well.

My brother, Rick, and I, along with our cousin, Pam, went home from those meetings armed with new game material. We would play "Oral Roberts" on our beds. Because Pam and I were two years older than four-year-old Rick and much more experienced in these matters, it was decided that I would be the evangelist, Pam the catcher, and Rick was always the boy with some mysterious illness. I'd put my hand on Rick's head, command, "Heal!" and then he would be "slain in the Spirit," with Pam catching him. But he never stayed down long. He was always "healed" and would pop back up, jumping up and down with us on the bed in great revelry as we dissolved into unabashed peals of laughter shouting, "Hallelujah! Hallelujah!"

***

It was these early experiences that influenced me. God had captivated my heart, and I loved to see His power at work. Little did I know, however, what His future plan was for me. His hand was shaping and molding me even then, but it would be a long, roundabout journey before He could get me to where He wanted me to be.

CHAPTER 3

The "No" Religion

"No, no, no! All you ever say is no," I snapped at my parents. "When I graduate, I'm going to live in the biggest city I can find where no one knows who I am…or cares! And I'll *never* marry a preacher!"

I stormed out of the parsonage kitchen and fled up to my room, my sanctuary where I could dream about being anything I wanted to be and doing anything I wanted to do. My rebellious anger seethed just under the surface of my teenage skin. I couldn't wait to graduate from high school, go to college, and have a career in a big city where I could get lost in the crowd. And that big city had a name—Los Angeles, California! I had never been there, and I didn't know how I was going to get there, but I was going to find a way.

When I was seven years old, we moved to another small town in Western Pennsylvania, where I spent the rest of my growing-up years. Situated about forty-five miles southwest of Pittsburgh, huddled within rolling farmland hills, I was convinced that it was the prototype for Mayberry from the "Andy Griffith Show." It had a well-defined downtown area with a Five-and-Ten Store, a bank, a post office, a musty old library, a drugstore with a soda fountain where the teenagers would gather after school, and a few other businesses that gave it that quaint, old-town feel. The streets were lined with large turn-of-the-century homes decked with wide, sweeping porches and surrounded by well-manicured lawns and massive ancient oak and elm trees that often pushed up the sidewalks with their long imposing root systems. The parks were the heartbeat of the town, where families would congregate after dinner on warm evenings to pick up a softball game until the dusk and streetlights shooed everyone home.

It was a safe town, and people cared about one another, and everyone knew each other…and each other's business. And herein lay the problem. My dad was the pastor of the only Pentecostal church in town, and everyone knew us. I felt like I was living in a giant glasshouse in the middle of Times Square. If my two brothers and I got out of line, my parents knew it before we even got home!

It seemed to me that the most difficult aspect of being Pentecostal back then was that there were an awful lot of rules to be followed. Being a PK (preacher's kid) meant having to always toe the line. The older I got, the wider the gap grew between my friends and me because of the things I was not allowed to do and places I was not allowed to go. When my friends would ask what our church believed, my answer was, "No dancing, no movies, no makeup, no jewelry, no smoking, no drinking, and no playing cards."

Usually the comeback would be something like, "That doesn't sound like much fun," and I was inclined to agree with them. So I dubbed it "The 'No' Religion."

I understood the Ten Commandments, and even living under the adjunct litany of those church-imposed "thou-shalt-nots" didn't really bother me either, except I had a *big* problem with the no-jewelry rule and the no-makeup thing. I was always a girly girl, and I loved that stuff (and still do). So in order to feed that fire, I would put makeup on in the bus going to school and take it off on my way home! Even though I gave my heart to Jesus, I didn't understand at that time that it was about a relationship with Him, not religious rules and regulations. I, therefore, bided my time until I could leave town and do whatever I wanted to do.

Aside from my chafing at the rules, however, I actually did have a wonderful childhood. My folks were good and loving people who felt that they were doing the best for us. As an adult, I realize why they limited some of those activities, but I surely didn't understand it then. Looking back now, I can see how valuable many of those lessons were to me. They served as foundational disciplines in my life. In 2 Corinthians 6:17–18 (NIV), we read, "Therefore come out from them and be separate, says the Lord." And Jesus said in John 15:19 (NIV), "...you do not belong to the world, but I have chosen you out of the world."

James 4:4–6 further states very clearly out of the New Living Translation, "Don't you realize that friendship with this world makes you an enemy of God? I say it again, that if your aim is to enjoy this world, you can't be a friend of God. What do you think the Scriptures mean when they say that the Holy Spirit, whom God has placed within us, jealously longs for us to be faithful? He gives us more and more strength to stand against such evil desires."

Yes, some of those noes exacted on us might have been a little extreme, and as time went on, they were somewhat relaxed, but it was important that I learned to stand strong against the opposing flow of the world. Basically, I was learning to swim upstream in the world's downhill current. God's borders are clearly defined, yet there's a lot of blurring and blending going on these days. Compromise causes us to lean closer in toward sin rather than closer to righteousness. We need to walk purely and righteously before God if we want to see revival and change take place in our personal lives, in the Church, and in the world. God says that He is holy, and therefore, we are to be holy.

Standing on the Inside

I pretty much had figured out what I could and couldn't do by the time I came into my early teens. The older I got, however, the more difficult it was to find the balance to try to fit in, when in actuality, I was supposed to be separate. I loved my parents, and I never wanted to jeopardize my dad's ministry nor did I want to be a reproach to Christ and my commitment to Him. It's just that I wanted to be like everyone else.

I asked Jesus into my heart when I was nine years old at a revival meeting in my home church. Dad would invite an evangelist to come once or twice a year to hold meetings every night for two weeks. It was at one of those services that I walked down the aisle of that church and made Jesus my Savior. I wept profusely as if I had been a hardened criminal and literally created a puddle of tears on the hand-hewn altar in front of the platform. The weight of God's glory was so strong that I couldn't contain it. It was the first indication (that I can remember) that God's hand was on me, and that's why I had the continual conflict going on inside of my heart as I got older. It was the age old raging warfare of flesh and spirit. I just didn't comprehend that my relationship with Jesus Christ would bring an obedience that would flow out of love for Him. I would learn that later. But at that time, I only saw it as rules and regulations, and subsequently, resentment and bitterness rose up in my heart. As the saying goes, I might have been sitting down on the outside, but I was standing up on the inside!

High school was really the most difficult time for me. In elementary school and junior high, I could pretty much blend in, but high school was different. It truly was a time of trials and separation. God's Word tells us we are never promised that, just because we are Christians, we will not have tribulations. As a matter of fact, the psalmist writes in Psalm 34:19 (NAS) that "many are the afflictions of the righteous." We don't get a free pass. However, that verse goes on to say, "But the LORD delivers him out of them all." The Lord is in the midst of the hard times even if we don't see His hand at work at that moment, and He will bring it around to our good if we trust Him. "And we know that all things work together for good to them that love God, to them who are the called according to his purpose" (Romans 8:28, KJV).

He would eventually restore all the things I hoped and longed for…and more. I just had to wait for His timing.

Cheerleader Fever

I had one major goal in school—I wanted to be a cheerleader. I tried out for junior varsity and varsity over the next four years but never made the squad. I couldn't figure it out. I could do all of the gymnastics and knew the cheers inside and out, so what was the problem? One of the older cheerleaders told me once that I wasn't chosen mainly because the cheerleaders sponsored the dances, which I wouldn't have been able to attend. Whatever the reason, I finally gave up in my senior year and didn't go to the cheer tryouts. But God knew my heart and disappointment and was working out a different plan.

I resigned myself to the fact that this was how things were going to be and was determined more than ever to go away to college and never marry a preacher or be in ministry or be anything that remotely resembled it. There was an old hymn that we used to sing in church entitled "I'll Go Where You Want Me to Go" (composers: Brown, Prior, and Rounsefell, 1892). The lyrics of the chorus are:

> I'll go where you want me to go, dear Lord,
> O'er mountain or plain or sea;
> I'll say what you want me to say, dear Lord,
> I'll be what you want me to be.

I wouldn't sing it. I viewed it as a prayer of surrender and submission to His will, and I wasn't willing to tell God I'd go anywhere He wanted me to go, because…well…I wasn't willing. I was afraid I would end up married to a preacher or—even worse—a missionary and would have to go to Africa and live in the jungle in a grass hut or go to India or China. We had missionaries who would come to the church and show slides of those kinds of things, and it scared me. No thank you! I had plans of my own.

The thing is, I wanted God's blessings, but I wanted them on my terms. I wanted Jesus to be Savior with my sins forgiven and on my way to Heaven, but I wasn't willing to let Him be Lord to whom I surrendered my whole will and life. Ultimately, I realized He wanted it all, everything, the whole enchilada of my life. The fact is if He's not Lord of all, He's not Lord at all. These many years later, I've found that total surrender to God has enriched my life so much that I can't understand why people don't want to serve Him! The benefits outweigh anything that this world has to offer.

I've Got Music

Music was my solace throughout my growing up years. It was one thing I excelled at and could get involved in. I pleaded with my parents for piano lessons when I was nine years old and loved it from day one. They never had to tell me to practice my lessons because I would literally play for hours. Actually, my brothers would beg me to stop playing!

Singing came naturally to me. From elementary school all the way to graduation, I belonged to the school choirs and small groups, and then into my adult years, I continued to sing in church choirs and community choral groups.

In the summer before my senior year, I performed with a Christian singing group made up of high school and college students. We toured throughout the Eastern United States, Great Britain, and mainland Europe in concert, sharing testimonies and praying with others. Little did I know that it would be training ground for my future ministry. The very thing I didn't want to do, i.e., be in ministry, was actually the very thing I did, except I didn't see it as such at the time. But I had to admit, I felt especially drawn to the altar time praying with others. God gently led me along long before I consciously knew it. Pay attention to the places He leads you. They could be markers along the way to your path of promise.

The Charismatic Movement

In the 1960s and '70s, a phenomenon swept across the United States and beyond known as the Charismatic Renewal Movement. Suddenly, folks in mainline church denominations were receiving the baptism of the Holy Spirit with the initial physical evidence of speaking in tongues. The term "charismatic" comes from the Greek word *charismata*, basically meaning "spiritual gift." Reports abounded of Episcopalians, Lutherans, Presbyterians, Mennonites, and Roman Catholics speaking in heavenly languages and encountering the manifestation of spiritual gifts such as prophecy, healings, and miracles.

All of this really puzzled the Pentecostals who, for fifty years, had held to the tenet of speaking in tongues and were often shunned and criticized for it. Now this Holy Spirit outbreak was being welcomed around the globe. The Pentecostal Movement had been birthed in 1910 out of the Azusa Street Revival in Los Angeles, and interestingly, the Charismatic Movement many years later, sprang up less than twenty miles away.

The Charismatic Movement began to gain momentum, and Pentecostalism, which was on the Protestant fringes, was now mainstream and eventually gave rise to the Jesus Movement, in which droves of young people who had joined the hippie counterculture gave their lives to Christ.

As I approached my late teens, the Charismatic Renewal was in full force, but I couldn't figure out what all the commotion was about. Those things happened in our churches regularly! However, the fact that it was now more accepted was good news to me. Up until then, we were often ridiculed and called "holy rollers," but now, we were cool. And because of its far-reaching appeal to the "un-churched," this renewal began to gradually relax many of the strict Pentecostal rules. People who were getting baptized in the Holy Spirit were not all living by the Pentecostals' codes of conduct, yet they were our brothers and sisters in Christ. It became an interesting dynamic and a major paradigm shift in many of the Pentecostal denominations.

As I said, the baptism in the Holy Spirit wasn't anything new to me. I received that infilling when I was eleven years old. It happened during a regular Sunday evening service when my friend Lisa* and I were praying at the altar. Lisa's sister-in-law came over to us and asked if we wanted to receive the Holy Spirit. Being eleven, I really didn't know what she meant exactly, but it sounded like a question that I was expected to respond to in the affirmative, so I said, "Yes." I found out just exactly what that meant about five minutes later! She began to pray over Lisa and me, and we both fell backward under the power of God, speaking in a language that we hadn't learned or understood. We stayed on the floor for about an hour, and while in the presence of the Lord, I had my first vision of Jesus.

I couldn't really make out His face, but I could see the long sleeve of His white robe draped down around His hand that was reaching out to me. I physically raised my hand toward Heaven to take hold of His, even though what I saw was in the spiritual realm.

---

* Name changed.

I eventually got up off the floor and sat in the front pew wondering what had happened to me. I said nothing about the vision to anyone. I didn't know what to make of it. Remarkably, however, Lisa said to me, "I had a vision of Jesus, and I saw Him holding your hand."

I didn't answer her because, frankly, I wasn't sure what to say, and neither did I mention that experience to anyone else for many years. I just didn't understand why I had had that vision, but even more, why Lisa would have the same vision. Years later, I realized that God's hand was at work in my life, and Lisa's vision served as a confirmation that it wasn't just my imagination.

God always confirms His word. In Deuteronomy 19:15b (NAS), we read, "…on the evidence of two or three witnesses a matter shall be confirmed."

Six years later, I would hear from Him again.

High School Senior Year

Like most high school senior years, mine was filled with the flurry of ACT/SAT tests, college applications, and the anticipation of a new chapter in my life. College meant freedom, and I couldn't wait to get there. I was accepted at the school where I had long wanted to attend, and the only thing left was the getting there.

I had my heart set on a degree in business administration. I prayed about it, and every sign seemed to point that direction. As far as going to a Bible school or being in ministry, I never heard the Lord speak to me concerning that at that time. He knew exactly how to deal with me. It had to be a process, a step-by-step; otherwise, I probably would have been like Jonah running in the opposite direction of Nineveh!

In the spring of that year, in the midst of finalizing my college plans, Dad had another evangelist come in to hold a revival meeting. This brother operated in the gift of prophecy, and I was absolutely spellbound as he pointed to certain individuals in the service, giving each one a word from the Lord that they confirmed was true.

Personal prophecy was new to me, and I was fascinated by it—that is, until he pointed to me.

That Sunday morning, as he was getting ready to preach, he stopped in the middle of his introduction and, from the platform, said, "Linda, I have a word for you from the Lord." I wasn't fascinated anymore—I was petrified! He went on, "The Lord wants you to know that He is holding your hand and directing you. He has marked your path and has a plan for your life." Among other things, he went on to say that my future belonged to Him. My mom, who sat next to me, grabbed my hand and started to cry while the rest of the congregation clapped and hallelujah-ed. And me? I was embarrassed to be singled out that morning. I wanted to slowly melt under the pew and stay there for the rest of the service until I could stealthily slither out the exit before anyone could stop and talk to me.

Today, when I receive a word from the Lord, I hallelujah with the best of them, but at that time, I was only seventeen. The idea that God would speak directly to me was a real fright. Personal prophecy, at that time, was not very common. But beyond that, there it was again—God was holding my hand. It really gave me pause. However, it also gave me peace and confidence. I felt that He was saying that I was moving in the right direction. What a relief! No African jungle! Now that was something I could hallelujah about!

Graduation Day finally came, and most of my friends boo-hooed, sad to leave their high school years behind. I didn't shed a tear. I didn't even go to a party to celebrate. I got into the car with my family and motored home with a smile on my face. My focus was on the coming September when I'd leave for college and "get out of Dodge." I felt as though I was reborn, ready to start a new life, and it couldn't come soon enough. My hopes were high. Things were looking up!

CHAPTER 4

Out of Dodge

From the first moment I stepped foot onto the grounds of Robert Morris College (now University) in Coraopolis, Pennsylvania, I embraced campus life with my whole being. I felt like I was home and never once regretted my decision to attend there. The first year of school was, as expected, difficult while I endeavored to acquaint myself with living on my own, making new friends and, of course, getting the rhythm of my academic studies. But what mattered most to me was that no one knew my origins nor did they care when they found out.

Brad

Brad Triska, a year older than I, had just transferred in from another college. While sitting with some friends in the cafeteria one day, he saw me enter through the glass doors. "See that girl over there? I'm going to marry her," he said with resolve as he stared after me. His friends laughed, but there was something deep inside him that just knew I was the one for him. Was it prophetic? Time would tell...

Beyond a shadow of a doubt, he felt we were to be together and began his campaign to pursue me. He called my dorm on several occasions to ask me out, but I continually turned him down. He would try to talk to me on campus and set up "chance" meetings, but I still kept my distance. I admit, *maybe* I was playing a little hard to get.

Some months later, on a cold, crisp afternoon, as winter tried to convince the autumn season to give up its long-standing hold, I walked across the campus to do some research at the library. Upon entering the building, I spotted Brad quietly studying alone at an obscure table in the corner. The library was crowded, and there weren't many seats available—but there was one. Yep, you guessed it. I selected my reading materials and asked Brad if I could sit down. We chatted a little and then went into our own study worlds. As I was getting ready to leave, he asked if I'd like a ride back to my dorm. The idea of crisscrossing the campus again in that blustery weather wasn't very appealing, and I gratefully accepted the offer.

We stepped out of the white-framed building and were greeted by the whip of wind as we made our trek to the parking area and piled into his fire engine red convertible Mustang with black interior and customized black pinstripes. She was hot! Brad said, "Hop in," and with the top down, he set the heater on full blast, handed me a blanket to put over my lap, and with music blaring and hair blowing, we whisked across the campus's rolling hills. We laughed and talked like two old friends as we motored toward the dorm. Maybe I was wrong about this guy…

The short jaunt to the dorm ended all too soon. I gathered my books, thanked him for the ride, and began to make my way out of the car.

"Wait," he said. "Look, I know we got off on the wrong foot, but please, will you go out with me?"

At first, I hesitated and then surprised myself when I said, "OK. Call me with details." I stepped out of the car and ran up the dorm steps in hopes that I had made the right decision.

Finding Jesus

That one date with Brad turned into another and another, but I had one hesitation. Although he had gone to parochial school and had even been an altar boy in the Catholic Church, he had never given his life to Christ. The Word of God says in 2 Corinthians 6:14 (NIV) that we are not to be "yoked together with unbelievers."

I tried to figure out a way to broach the subject with him. I knew our relationship could go no further until he became a follower of Christ. If I had to, I was prepared to tell him good-bye.

One January afternoon upon return from winter break, I asked Brad if he would drive me to the shopping plaza a few miles away. Winter was in full swing by then, and there was a soft snow falling. We slowly crept along the slick roads, but I didn't pay much attention to the winter wonderland outside. I was preoccupied with my own thoughts of how to get the opportunity to introduce Brad to Jesus. I had no idea how he would respond, but I had to find out. However, my concerns were for naught. The Holy Spirit was already at work.

I made my purchases at the plaza, and we returned to the students' parking lot. Brad switched the ignition off and turned toward me.

"Before you go," he said, "I want to ask you a question." As he searched my eyes intently, he asked, "What is it about you that makes you so different? I've never met anyone like you. What is it?"

Bingo! There was the very open door for which I had waited and prayed! People really do watch our lives, and if we live the life Christ has called us to live, it will be apparent to others without uttering a word. We will win more people with our actions than with our words.

His question really surprised me, but I quickly rushed through that open door and replied, "What you see in me, Brad, is Jesus," and from there, I proceeded to share the Gospel with him.

He listened attentively without interruption. He was so quiet that I wondered if I had gotten through to him. When I had finished, my words hung in the dead silence of the car. Finally, he remarked, "No one has ever explained that to me quite that way before." I could see he was contemplating what I had said. But the real question was did he actually understand it, and was he willing to take the step of faith to salvation?

I couldn't stand the suspense anymore and just asked him point blank, "Do you want to ask the Lord into your heart?" Then I held my breath.

Here's what we need to realize when we share the Good News—we can't save anyone! That is solely the work of the Holy Spirit. Our job is to witness, to tell others about the saving grace of Jesus Christ. Then it's the Holy Spirit's job to convict and bring to salvation. If their answer is no, they are not rejecting us. They are rejecting God's free gift through His Son who died for us and rose again. If the answer is yes, however, we have literally snatched them from the fires of hell (see Jude 1:23). But the onus is on them. We will *all* stand alone before God one day and have to answer the question, "What did you do with Jesus? Did you accept Him or reject Him?"

And what was Brad's answer? It was a very simple, "Yes." Just yes. No theological discussions. No arguments. No additional questions. I even asked him if he had any questions, but he said, "No, I understand. I always felt there was something more but didn't know what it was," and with that, he asked what he needed to do. That was it. The Holy Spirit had already prepared Brad's heart.

So on that cold, January afternoon, while we sat in the red Mustang, parked in the student lot with the snow softly falling outside around us, I led Brad in the sinner's prayer, and he became a new creation in Christ, born into the Kingdom of Heaven.

Cheerleader Fever Relapse

Life on campus fell into a routine of classes, studies, and dates with Brad, but I had one more ax to grind. I spied a notice for cheerleader auditions, and I just had to give it one more try. I felt that the playing field was now level, and maybe, I would have a fair chance. I had to find out.

I went to the meetings and the practices and on to the tryouts. I prayed and asked God for His will (hoping it would be the same as mine!) and His favor one last time before I headed to the gymnasium for the final results. This was the big day! Each candidate had one last opportunity to perform, and then we all sat in the bleachers to wait and hope our name would be called.

There were dozens of girls there for the tryouts, most of whom had been cheerleaders in high school. They had experience, I had none. And to make things more interesting, there were only five openings to fill. What in the world was I thinking? What chance did I have? I was really nervous and about ready to bolt from the gym as other girls' names were called, but wait…what? Whose name was just called? Everyone was looking at me and clapping and congratulating me. I made it! Not only that, I was the only one who had not been a cheerleader in high school. To me, it was miraculous!

When I think about it even now, I'm amazed how the Lord cared even about a young girl's dream. God's answers are yes, no, or wait. This was a dream that required a wait before a yes. Again, we have to trust that He will bring everything to our good according to His will and purposes and at the right time. I love the fact that He cares about the little things that concern us. I've heard some saints comment that they don't want to bother God with what they deem as small things, but I have great news—He wants to be bothered! He wants us to bring everything to Him, both the large and small things in our lives. He is a loving Father and only wants the best for us, even when we don't understand why some things happen the way they do. We just have to trust that He knows what's best, and that He is in control of every situation.

I loved being a cheerleader. By my senior year, I was captain of the cheer squad, something I wouldn't have ever expected or dared to dream. But God had even more in store, more than I could have ever imagined.

A Year to Remember

My senior year was hectic, yet it was one of the most amazing years of my life. Besides the cheer practices, games, and my studies, I had to prepare to do my student teaching in the spring semester. I had decided to get my teaching certification so that I would have the option of either teaching business subjects or going into the business world.

The holidays came, and Brad and I made plans to celebrate New Year's Eve together. He made reservations at The Edge Restaurant that sat at the pinnacle of Mount Washington, high above downtown Pittsburgh, boasting a spectacular panoramic view of the city.

The cold night began to yield a sparkling snow to herald in the New Year, adding to the romance and enchantment of the night. It was here that Brad proposed, and I said yes.

My mind reeled back to the declaration he had made four years before. "I'm going to marry that girl." Truly, God was in the details.

We arranged to get married that summer after I graduated. Brad had already graduated and was job hunting. In the midst of everything else, I now had a wedding to plan.

Above and Beyond

I began my student teaching right after we returned from winter break teaching business subjects. I would teach for four days and, on Fridays, returned to my college classes. One afternoon, upon my return from the high school, there was a note from the director of activities tacked on my dormitory door with a request to meet with him. Mystified, I called and made an appointment for the following Friday. I knew him from several activities that he and I had been involved with over the past four years. We were on a first name basis, and I was comfortable sitting in his office that afternoon but certainly was not prepared for what he was about to say.

He started with, "Linda, there's an opportunity that we, the administration, would like to present to you."

Now my curiosity was piqued. I like the word "opportunity." To me, it holds promise and adventure. I was all ears.

He went on, "The State of Pennsylvania is searching for finalists to compete in the Miss Pennsylvania/Miss USA Pageant, and we would like to enter you. You will hold the college title and will represent the school as our entrant, and of course, we will cover all of the entry fees. The competition is in March if you choose to accept."

I was stunned and honestly couldn't answer him for a long moment. I never saw that one coming! The school had never before submitted an entrant in a state beauty pageant. I was the first and felt so honored. When I was finally able to somewhat recover my voice, I asked, "Why me? Why not this year's homecoming queen?"

He rather matter-of-factly answered, "Because we believe in you and would be proud to have you represent us."

So there it was. I accepted the offer in a dreamy fog and was conferred with the title of "Miss Robert Morris College," just like that. I left his office dazed, excited, frightened, and everything in between and wondered how I was going to fit everything into my schedule. But one thing for sure, I was not going to miss an opportunity of a lifetime like this!

Brad and my family and friends were excited for me and supported me with whatever assistance they could lend. It all became a nonstop whirl of activity.

Although thrilled to be there, I was also nervous. I had no idea what to expect. Many of those girls had grown up competing in pageants and had coaches to get them to the title. Again, what was I doing there? But once things began to take off, there was no time to think about that. I just went for the ride.

The pageant was held in Washington, Pennsylvania, and we girls were housed in a hotel close by. A chaperone was assigned to every four girls, and we could do nothing—and I mean nothing—without our chaperone. Our phone calls were monitored, and they observed how we behaved in all situations. That was part of the scoring and judging. What we wore, how we handled ourselves in the judges' interviews, how we interacted with the other girls, and how we presented ourselves to the media, which was around all of the time, was all part of the judging. Opinions were being formed throughout the extended weekend. We did a lot of public relations and were paraded around to several special events, all being covered by the news. We took photos with several state and local officials, signed autographs, and did a ton of waving. I smiled and waved and walked tall and was polite and had a super duper great time! It was an event that I would long bask in the memory of—a definite highlight of my life.

The final competition night arrived. The auditorium was full, and I could see my family, fiancé, and friends in the center section, rooting for me beyond the stage floor lights. The first runway event was the parade of costumes where each of us was introduced as we wore our title sash and a costume that represented that title. Because

Robert Morris's mascot was a colonial man, that's what I chose as my costume.

Next was the swimsuit competition. Those were the days when one-pieces were required. I wore a simple black suit with black pumps. My heart pumped too when they called my name, and I had to walk that runway as if I had all of the poise in the world. Yeah, right!

And lastly, the most popular event, was the gown competition. I had designed an empire-waist, green organza, full-length gown and had dyed my shoes green to match. It was *the* moment, and I glided down the runway one more time amid the cheers of my adherents.

The Miss Pennsylvania Pageant gown competition.

Now came the moment of reckoning. Third runner-up is—no, not my name. Second runner-up—no, not my name either. And the winner of the new Miss Pennsylvania title is—the same gal who won the Pittsburgh United Way Miss Torch Pageant the summer before.

Okay, so I wasn't the winner, but honestly, I felt like a winner just being selected to be there. I wasn't all that distraught. It was an amazing experience, and I just felt so very blessed to be a part of it. It was a wonderful adventure that most girls would never get the opportunity to experience, and I viewed it as the grand finale of my college days.

Throughout my college years, the Lord was so gracious to give me the desires of my heart.

His Word promises in Psalm 145:19 (NIV), "He fulfills the desires of those who fear him." I have seen it work in my life, not only in this instance, but throughout the subsequent years. Ephesians 3:20 (NIV) declares, "Now to him who is able to do immeasurably more than all we ask or imagine, according to his power that is at work within us…" He fulfilled my desires and then gave me more than I asked for or could even dream up. God saw an ordinary girl dream impossible dreams, and He not only fulfilled those dreams, but gave her exceedingly and abundantly more than she asked. God is the dream giver. He gives us the dream and then works it out to bring it to pass. I say to you, "Dream!" and dream *big*, for there is *nothing* impossible with God!

Although so many of my prayers were being answered during that time, I admit that I was not growing spiritually. I was busy and had my own agenda, doing all of the things *I* wanted to do. I prayed my "gimme" nighttime prayers, but there was no substantial spiritual increase or an "I-surrender-all" moment…not yet. The Lord was gracious to let me run, but the time was coming when He would call an all-in, and I would have a choice to make.

My college years came to a close when I graduated in May, and this time, I shed a ton of tears. Yes, I would miss the joys and excitement of those four years, but I also looked forward to turning the page of a new chapter in my life. I had a wedding and lifetime to plan.

CHAPTER 5

White Lace and Promises

Brad had graduated a semester ahead of me. Once he had received his degree, he began job hunting in earnest. During his junior and senior years, he was hired on with Gulf Oil as a gas station attendant on the Pennsylvania Turnpike. His intent was to work for Gulf Oil in their marketing department upon graduation. Unfortunately, those were the years when oil took a downturn, and even though he was able to attain an interview with a vice president, he was told they couldn't guarantee his future with them since they were already starting to lay employees off. He was disappointed but decided to remain at the gas station until he could secure something more permanent. We had set a wedding date for late August of that year, and plans were already in motion. We became more concerned about employment and prayed more fervently. But God was working behind the scenes.

On a mild afternoon in April, Brad was on shift at the station when a gentleman pulled in for service. Brad waited on him, filling up his gas tank, checking his oil, and cleaning the windshield. (What happened to those days?) The gentleman gave him his credit card for payment, and Brad noticed it was a company card for Kellogg's Cereal Company. That caught his attention!

"How do you get a job with a company like this?" he queried.

The man smiled and stated offhandedly, "Well, Son, you need a degree."

"I do have a degree! I just graduated with a business degree in marketing." He peered at the gentleman hopefully.

"Oh. All right then, here's my business card. If you like, you can send your resume to me at this address. We don't have any openings right now, but we'll keep your resume on file in case anything becomes available." Other than a brief "thank you," nothing else was said, and the gentleman sped off, disappearing into the turnpike traffic.

Brad studied the name on the business card—Jim Reynolds*, Assistant Division Manager—then shoved the card into his uniform pocket and resolved to send his resume the next day. It was a long shot, but he wasn't going to leave any stone unturned.

Later that evening, however, an unusual thing happened. The pay phone in the station office rang. That was strange. No one ever called in on the pay phone. The employees only used it to call out. One of the attendants tenuously answered. The gentleman on the other end gave his name and said he had met a young station attendant that afternoon and wanted to speak to him. Not knowing his name, he described a person who could only have been Brad.

Surprised, Brad picked up the phone and realized it was Jim Reynolds from Kellogg's. Jim stated that an unanticipated opening had just become available in the sales department, and if Brad was interested, he should come to Youngstown, Ohio, for an interview. Arrangements were made to meet the following evening. Brad hung the phone up, more than a little wonderstruck.

The next evening, Brad drove to Ohio during a raging thunderstorm. He wasn't sure what to make of it all, but with a quick prayer, ventured out into the inclement weather.

The interview went well, and he learned the story of how this sudden job opening had appeared. Jim unexpectedly had to dismiss the Youngstown-area sales representative that very day. Now he had an opening to fill and immediately thought about the young man he had had a conversation with that afternoon at the gas station.

A week later, Jim called Brad and asked if both he and I would be willing to meet the division manager for dinner. He explained that the division manager liked to make sure the spouses were supportive

---

* Name changed.

of the employee's career. Little did I know at the time that "supportive" meant willing to be transferred all around the country. Well, we must have passed muster, and the rest is history. Brad was hired in May and began his twenty-three-year-long career with Kellogg's starting out as a sales representative.

To this day, we do not know how Jim got the phone number for that pay phone or how he happened to drive into that gas station on that day and how Brad happened to be on duty at that moment. It couldn't have been anything else but orchestrated by the hand of God!

Big Hopes, Big Dreams

On August 25th of that year, I became Mrs. Bradley Triska. We were married in my home church, where my dad was senior pastor. Dad walked me down the aisle then officiated the rest of the ceremony. We were excited for our lives to begin.

Once we moved to Ohio, I began my own job hunt. Armed with my business degree and a stack of resumes, I was ready to set the world on fire. After student teaching, I decided that I really didn't want to teach high school, and I set my sights on finding employment in a corporation. However, my teacher's training would serve me well in the years to come. It's amazing how God is able to redeem everything. Teaching would be one of those redemptions for me, but I wouldn't find that out until a long time later.

I finally determined that what I really wanted was a management position in the human resources (HR) department of a large corporation. At that time, it was my big dream, and once again, it was more about, "God, this is what I want." I really didn't ask what He wanted, but I was soon to find out just what His thoughts were about that.

I constantly perused the classified section of the newspaper searching for that perfect job. One evening, a few months into my quest, I spotted an ad for an executive administrative assistant to the president of a major manufacturing corporation. My wheels began to turn. Maybe if I could get hired by this company, I could work for the president for a time and then try to figure my way into the HR department. I decided to give it a shot and applied.

About a week later, I got a call for an interview. I met the president in the executive suites on the top floor of their high-rise corporate headquarters. The interview seemed to go well, and I began to hope and pray. *"Please, Lord,"* I said as I headed down the highway on my way back home. *"I want that job! It sounds so perfect for me, and there's so much opportunity there to move up!"*

I was called in for a second interview, this time with the HR vice president. Great! It gave me a chance to get on his radar screen, too. I left the interview on what I felt was a positive note and went home to wait for their decision.

After about a month of waiting, I got the call...the job was mine!

I started my new job a few weeks later. I tried to immerse myself not only in mastering the position but also worked to educate myself on the business itself. I read everything on the subject that I could find. It paid off down the road.

Having a position in the executive suites had its perks, particularly since I worked for the president. Just to work side by side with sharp-minded executives was a bonus in and of itself. There was so much I learned from them by association.

Spiritual Waterloo

I worked for the president for approximately a year before I began to get bored with the position. I needed more challenge and still had my eye on human resources. Ron*, HR Vice President, and I had forged a nice working relationship. He was professional, yet friendly and approachable, but I had not heard about any open positions in his department, and I just wasn't sure how to broach the subject. In contrast, my boss, Gerald**, was very closed off and distant. I

---

* Name changed.
** Name changed.

didn't feel that I could go to him either and ask about my future with the company. I felt stuck.

The New Year arrived with its usual dank and cold weather. The trees were stark with their bare branches lifted up to the monotonous grey sky and looked as dreary as the weather itself. The depressing landscape mirrored my own somber mood as I drove to work that Monday morning. I needed to somehow navigate my way out of my present position and move into HR's management training program, an entry-level program designed as an on-the-job training course for those the corporate powers deemed to have potential for upward mobility.

There has to be a way, Lord. Please open a door for me, I silently prayed as I pulled my car into the employees' parking lot.

I made my way up to my office and poked my head into my boss's office to see what the day's calendar held. Oddly, he wasn't there. Though he traveled a great deal of the time, he usually came in on Mondays to tie up loose ends before leaving again.

As I settled myself at my desk, the phone rang. It was Ron from HR. He said he needed to see me in his office immediately. I knocked on his door and was motioned in to take a seat. He looked troubled, almost austere, not the usual lighthearted Ron I knew. He cut right to the chase.

"Linda, I need to tell you something," he said with gravity. "Gerald has been accused of insider trading and is under investigation by the Securities and Exchange Commission. These are very serious allegations, and it has already somehow leaked out to the media. You are not to speak to the press, or to anyone else for that matter, concerning this situation. Should you receive calls from the media, you are to field them to me. At this point, we do not know where Gerald is. So I need to ask you—and you must be honest—do you know anything about the allegations or know Gerald's whereabouts?"

My eyes had to have been as big as silver dollars. I shook my head in the negative. I had no idea on either count. My final instructions were to call Ron immediately if Gerald should come in.

I left Ron's office with my mind in a dither. I racked my brain trying to remember if I had missed anything with any of the stock transactions. I couldn't think of a thing.

As if right on cue, my phone started to ring incessantly, and yes, it was the press sniffing around like hounds on the hunt for details about the already-leaked-out story. Obediently, I fielded those calls to HR. I also got calls from staff members hoping for additional information to flesh out the sketchy pieces of hearsay that whirled around the company at tornado speed. I warded them all off the best I could and went home that evening exhausted.

Gerald never did come in on Monday or Tuesday nor did he call. By then, things got frantic. I was questioned over and over by the CEO and VPs, but I had no new information. Then on Tuesday afternoon, things came to a head. I received a call from one of the VPs at the main corporate office. He angrily interrogated me as to Gerald's whereabouts, but I could only give him the same answer that I had given everyone else: I didn't know.

I'm not sure why they thought I harbored information, but obviously they thought I did.

At that point, he completely lost his temper and shouted across the phone line, "Young lady, you had better tell me the truth as to where he is or you are going to be in a great deal of trouble!" I still had no answers. He slammed the phone down and the line went dead.

My stomach was in knots and my head pounded. I searched my memory for anything that may have been said in a long-forgotten conversation that might give a clue. Then…I had an idea.

A few minutes later, the phone rang again. This time it was from Sherry*, the administrative assistant to the VP who has just railed at me. Sherry tried to sweet-talk me in hopes of gleaning some information. I guess she thought she'd win me over with a little honey. I was tired of the badgering. Wearily, I said, "Sherry, I really and truly don't know where Gerald is. However, I know he sometimes flies down south on weekends and goes sailing on his yacht. Maybe that's where he is. Perhaps someone should call the coastguard."

That bit of information must have set the wheels in motion because when I got in the next morning, Gerald was there lying in wait for me. He called me into his office, and he was irate! He leveled a tongue-lashing against me that, to this day, I have not forgotten. He ranted and raved about how I had been disloyal, having turned him in and that I would get my just desserts. Evidently, my suspicions were correct. He had sailed his yacht into international waters, and the authorities caught up with him.

He then lowered his voice and nefariously stated that I too could be implicated! What? I had nothing whatever to do with those allegations. There wasn't a modicum of truth to his suggestion, but I still panicked. My mind tried to trace back to any paperwork I had prepared that could possibly implicate me. There was nothing. By all accounts, I was innocent. I think he wanted to inflict pain by frightening me as he felt that I had betrayed him; and I bought it—hook, line, and sinker. I was shaken to the core.

In a final noxious blast at the end of his red-faced diatribe, he bellowed, "And you're fired! Now get out!"

I was numb. I stumbled out of his office in a blur of tears, packed up my personal belongings, and headed down the hall to make one last stop. I knocked on Ron's door and crumbled into shreds of emotion in his office. Briefly, I stammered out what had happened.

"Look," he comforted, "first of all, Gerald can't fire you. Only I can, and frankly, I don't choose to at this point. I'll tell you what. You go home for a few days—with pay—until I can sort this out. I'll call you when I get it straight."

I went back down the same stairs that I had mounted a half hour earlier and staggered out into the shivering elements. Climbing into my car, I sat behind the wheel until I was able to stop shaking and pull myself together for the drive. There was slush and ice on the roads, and I had to steel my thoughts until I arrived home.

I carefully steered my car into the garage of the home we had bought a year earlier. It had been a fixer-upper, to be sure, but we had slowly remodeled it to our taste over the previous year. Brad and I had worked hard to saved our money so we could turn the pristine little white-frame house into our home. Now what were we going to do? We needed my salary to help pay the bills.

I dropped the box of personal belongings from my desk onto the kitchen table and made my way down the hall to our bedroom. There, I collapsed onto the bed, brokenhearted, still stinging from all of the tirades I had received over the past couple of days and wept until there were no more tears to be shed. I thought of all the plans I had made, my dreams of having a successful career in human resources in corporate America all dissolving like the salt-riddled ice on the roads I had just maneuvered. I worried about the bills that would now have to be paid on one salary. I was horrified at the thought of telling Brad and our families and friends that I had been fired from this great job. And I was terrified at the thought of the Securities and Exchange Commission coming after me.

"*God, how could this have happened? You gave me this job!*" I cried.

When Brad arrived home, I choked out the whole sordid fiasco. I could barely articulate my words due to the fresh batch of tears that welled up once again. He tried to console me. "We'll figure it out, Honey," he reassured me, but I could tell that he wasn't quite so convinced himself.

I slept fitfully that night with strange dreams dancing in and out of my slumber. I stumbled out of bed the next morning, helped Brad get ready for work, and then had the solitude of my house in which to think, cry, pray. The new snow that lazily drifted down that morning only added to my dismal state.

By afternoon, I had had it with my melancholy. To distract myself, I lay down on the living room sofa and began to read a book my parents had given me. They used to supply me with books about the Charismatic Movement and testimonies of those who had mind-boggling spiritual experiences and supernatural encounters. I would avidly devour them.

The book I was in the midst of reading that day was Pat Robertson's *Shout It from the Housetops*. It was the account of the birth of the Christian Broadcasting Network (CBN) and was chock-full of God-sized miracles. I read it all the way to the end that afternoon. But rather than it encouraging me, the story upset me. To be honest, it provoked me to spiritual jealousy. I slammed it shut and hurled it across the room. Nothing I had seen up to that point in my life matched up to some of those outrageous, miraculous accounts.

"*God,*" I cried out. "*I don't hear your voice, and I haven't seen these kinds of miracles in my life, and if I ever needed one, I need one now!*"

Brad and I were faithful church attendees, paid our tithes, and were active in different ministries. Together, we worked with the youth group, and I was in the choir and directed the dramas. We were busy in the house of the Lord, but the Lord was clearly after something much more than that. I knew something was amiss.

Frustrated and shattered, I slipped to my knees and laid it all out before God. I sobbed out my disappointments and heartaches to Him. I told Him that I, too, wanted to hear His voice and see miracles in my life, like the ones I read about in those books. The Holy Spirit was obviously drawing me and setting me up for what God really wanted to do in my life.

And then something happened. The atmosphere became charged with the presence of the Holy Spirit. I began to pray aloud in tongues—something I hadn't done in a long time—and, immediately afterward spoke the interpretation of that heavenly language in English. I was astonished! I had never interpreted a message in tongues before that.

The word was: "If you will surrender your whole heart and life to me, you will surely see miracles." He had more to say. He asked me to give Him everything and allow Him to do the work that He wanted to do in me because He wanted to use me for His glory.

I knew exactly what that prophetic word meant. I knew I had avoided His will and wanted things my own way. From our human perspective, to surrender everything to Him is a terrifying prospect until we realize that He does all for our good. To relinquish my agenda to Him would take faith, and a lot of it, but I had nowhere else to go. I felt as though my whole life was on the line. My plans had led me to a brick wall. The only place to run was into Jesus's arms, and that's exactly where He wanted me to be.

There's an alluring scripture that speaks about this issue of God's call to us to surrender to Him. I love the way The Living Bible says it: "Yet the Lord still waits for you to come to him, so he can show you his love; he will conquer you to bless you, just as he said. For the Lord is faithful to his promises. Blessed are all those who wait for him to help them" (Isaiah 30:18).

He wants to conquer our desires and wishes and exchange them for His. There is great blessing in that. It's a win-win situation. God has created each of us for a certain purpose, but we need to let Him have His way in our lives and surrender all to Him, otherwise, we are in rebellion, not obedience. Being in the center of the Father's will, will bring great peace, joy, and blessing.

I turned it all over in my mind, and He waited...waited for the answer that He had wanted to hear for a long time. Finally, with hands raised and tears streaming down my cheeks, I surrendered everything to Him. Jesus became not only my Savior but also King Jesus, my Lord. I told Him that I did not know why He wanted me, but if there was something He could do with me, I was all His. I felt Him welcome me home like the prodigal son and peace rolled over me. I knew that everything would be all right...somehow.

When I think of that day, I equate it to the 1815 Battle of Waterloo. Waterloo was the decisive end of the rule of French emperor, Napoleon Bonaparte, who was completely defeated and exiled to St. Helene Island until his death. My stubborn self-will met its Waterloo that January day, and I exchanged it for His will. But the great thing about our Father is He doesn't exile us. He rebuilds us and moves us toward His purposes for His glory.

I wish I could say that I became perfect and did everything right from that moment forward, but I can't. However, I was finally on the right track and headed in His direction, and the Lord began a new work in me. For the first time in my life, I was eager to follow His lead.

I had hoped Ron would call that day, but he didn't; nor did he call the next day, which put me into the weekend. It felt endless, but I had put everything into the Lord's hands and had to trust that whatever came about was His will.

Early Monday morning, the call finally came. Ron sounded chipper, like the old Ron I knew. I held my breath as to the verdict. "Linda, I've worked everything out. You're in the clear."

I was so relieved. Thank you, Jesus! It was great news in itself just to be cleared of any wrongdoing, but he had more, and herein was my second miracle.

"So," he went on, "How would you like to come and work for me in HR?" I was shocked! "We'd like to put you in the management training program in human resources. How does that sound?" Jesus conquered me to bless me with not one miracle, but two.

Winds of Change

I reported to my new manager a few days later, eager to get started. The human resources department was split into two divisions, personnel and labor relations. In order to give me an overall picture, I bounced between the two. I really enjoyed the labor relations side. It exposed me to the manufacturing and union relations. Learning about the manufacturing and business side of the company in my earlier position had worked to my benefit.

Many of my projects necessitated going inside the factory. I had my own hard hat, goggles, steel-toed shoes, and a zip-up jumpsuit that were mandatory wear when in the plant. It was a rush to stroll down the aisles of that oversized world that teemed with looming, thunderous machines tirelessly pushing out product.

The Lord had given me favor with my supervisors, and I relished going to work every day. He had even given me peace with my former boss, Gerald, as well. One day in the cafeteria, he made his way over to me, asked how I was doing, and gave me a hug! I think it was his way of an apology, but I held no animosity toward him and had already forgiven him. Unforgiveness is unnecessary baggage that doesn't need to be lugged around. It's a personal choice to hold a grudge and not forgive, and it only hurts the one who carries it. God's Word says that if we don't forgive others, He can't forgive us. Anyway, why would I hold a grudge? The dictates of those circumstances created my miracle giving me the desires of my heart.

Months later, the rumor was that Gerald had been convicted of the crime and served prison time. My hope is that he found Jesus there.

I immediately made changes in my spiritual life to keep my promise to the Lord. If I surrendered all, I needed to make Him number one in my life and spend more time getting to know Him intimately. Prior to this, I didn't have a consistent daily devotional time. Bible study was hit-and-miss at best, and my prayer life was more of what I call "drive-by prayers"—you know, like driving up to a fast-food window and giving the attendant your order: "One salvation and two healings, please."

I knew God wanted more from me than that, so I set aside more time to read the Word and be on my knees in prayer, including time for worship and praise. As a result, the Word began to open up and made more sense to me than ever before. It was as if the Holy Spirit became my personal tutor. I also began to hear the voice of the Lord and "know" things by the inspiration of the Spirit. The first time that took place, however, I didn't even recognize it.

It happened during a Sunday morning service. Our pastor at the time shared with the congregation about the vacation he and his family had just returned from in Ireland. It was general information about places they had visited, the beauty of the land, the warmth of the people, and so on.

Out of the blue, I whispered to Brad, "They are going to move to Ireland to be missionaries."

He turned to me and whispered back, "Why on earth would you say that?"

"I don't know," I replied, just as puzzled about my remark as he was. But I was convinced and somehow just knew.

Our pastor and family had been at that church for several years, and there was no indication of a change that would have prompted me to think that.

Three Sunday mornings later, during the church service, the pastor asked his family to join him on the platform. He then read a letter of resignation and went on to explain, "After visiting Ireland, my family and I fell in love with the people and the country, and we feel that God has called us to be missionaries there."

The congregation was in shock, but no one more than I! Brad and I whipped our heads toward each other in amazement. Brad quietly asked, "How did you know?"

Perplexed, I answered him with the same profound answer that I had given him before, "I don't know!"

In the course of time, I would realize that this "knowing" is called the gift of the word of knowledge, one of the gifts of the Holy Spirit as outlined in 1 Corinthians 12:8, and this was the beginning of God's preparation for the calling He had on my life.

We were sad to see our pastor and family leave. They had become personal friends of ours. However, I was soon to find out that the winds of change were blowing in our direction as well.

It was just about a year after I began my new position in HR and about a month after our pastor's resignation that Brad came home from work and looked a little nervous. I could see he had something on his mind but was hesitant to put it out there. We sat down to dinner, and I happily chattered about my day, but he was uncharacteristically quiet and apparently distracted.

I finally had enough of the mystery and flat out asked him, "OK, so what's going on?"

He put his fork down and looked straight at me. "I need to tell you something."

Obviously!

"I've just been offered a job promotion. They want to move us to Savannah, Georgia."

CHAPTER 6

In the Heart of Dixie

The color drained out of my face. He couldn't be serious! Not now! I always knew there was a possibility that we could get transferred someday, but God had given me this awesome job now; I was making really good money, and I was so happy. I had finally made some inroads into my career. Surely, He wouldn't ask me to give it up now when everything was going so great. Or would He? Where was Savannah, Georgia, anyhow?

Brad's words cut through my thoughts. He all of a sudden became animated and outlined all the great things that would come with the move. He'd become an accounts manager with a larger territory, and the company would pay for the whole move, which included packers to pack up the house, and he'd get a big fat raise along with a bonus and a new company car, and...

"And I have to give up my career," I flatly finished his sentence.

The light and excitement went out of his eyes. He looked down. "Well, you could get another job there..." His voice trailed off. He knew he was asking a lot of me. After a moment, he continued, "Listen, we have to make this decision together. If you decide you don't want to do this, then we won't. The only thing is that if I turn this down, I'll probably have to find another job because Kellogg's wants people they can move up and groom for management. Transferring them around the country, and sometimes to other countries, is the way they do it. They want their managers to understand all markets."

So the bottom line was that if we chose to take this first move, we had to be all in because, more than likely, there would be more transfers in the future if the company put him on their radar, as they obviously had. It was pretty much a career-long commitment, and if we decided to go that way, it was blaringly apparent that I would not be able to pursue my own corporate career. I'd be on Kellogg's timetable. I could get started again in another company, but the same thing would probably happen if Brad was reassigned.

"Oh, and…umm…I have to give an answer in a couple of days or it's off the table."

Poor Brad! He tried to be fair. He obviously wanted to accept that promotion, yet he knew I loved my job too and was also slotted for management. The question came down to: do we follow his career or mine? Then there was the question about having a family. Did I want to work after we had kids or be a stay-at-home mom? In two days, we had to make a decision for our entire future.

I excused myself from the table and headed to our bedroom to seek God for direction. This decision was just way too big for me to make without His guidance.

God, what do I do now? You gave me this job. You've given me favor with the company. I'm on my way up. Surely, you're not telling me to give up all of my dreams, are you? I anguished in prayer, desperate for a fast answer, and yet, dreading what I might hear. Right away, I heard the voice that I was learning to recognize…only I was already not happy with what I heard. I decided I was too tired and upset at that point to get a good answer, and so, like Scarlett O'Hara in *Gone with the Wind*, I resolved that I'd think about it tomorrow.

I tried to be my sunny self the next day at work, attempting to hide the duplicity of what was really going on inside. It was difficult to concentrate on the job at hand when I kept hearing the Lord ask, "Will you surrender your will to mine?" There it was—God's test of my will against His. Would I hold up my end of the bargain?

I turned the key in the back door of the house at the end of my work day. Brad hadn't gotten home yet, and it was just God and me. He asked again, "Will you surrender your will to mine?" I struggled and wrestled and rationalized and cried. He was asking me to surrender my dreams for His. If I did, I would have to walk away from everything that I had struggled to achieve, and more than likely, as I saw it, the loss of my career would be forever. But if I didn't surrender to Him, then I was, in effect, placing my will and dreams on a throne above God, which would make them idols in my life.

In Dr. Bruce Wilkinson's excellent book, *The Dream Giver*, he states, "But the time will come when God asks you to surrender the Dream itself. Often, He'll ask you to take a very tangible step to seal your decision. That could be selling or giving something away, signing a contract, moving, or even resigning."[2] I was at that very crossroad. God asked me to surrender my dream and trust and follow Him into the unknown.

When Brad came through the door that evening, I could tell that he was heavy-hearted, too. He wanted that promotion, but he wanted me to be happy as well. We discussed it long into the night while I continued to hear, "Will you surrender your will to mine?"

There was just no other answer, and I finally relinquished, "Yes, Lord. I'll go where You want me to go. I'll trust You." That was exactly what He wanted to hear. God will never lord it over us. He calls and will give us a nudge but ultimately leaves the choice to us. I had made a promise to go His way. How could I take it back? For one, it felt that my very integrity was at stake; and two, I really did want to be obedient. Obedience is the path to the miraculous, and I wanted to see miracles in my life. For me, there was just no other answer.

Once we made that decision, Brad contacted his district office and gave them the go-ahead. The deed was done, and things began to move at a rapid pace. Within a week, Brad left for Savannah to train in his new job. I put the house on the market, and it sold in three days! I took it as a sign that God was definitely orchestrating this. Our parents weren't happy about our 800-mile-away move but gave us their blessing amidst a fountain of tears.

The thing I dreaded most was giving the news to my immediate boss, but I knew I had to do that quickly as I was booked to fly to Savannah shortly to house hunt. The day I walked into his office to

---

2   Bruce Wilkinson, *The Dream Giver*, (Sisters Oregon: Multnomah Publishers) p. 133

give my two-week's notice, I wished I was anywhere but there. I had typed out a letter of resignation and handed it to him.

He read it, let out a huge sigh, and said, "Sit down. What's going on here?"

He heard me out as I disclosed the transfer and our time schedule, then folded his hands in front of him, peered over the rim of his reading glasses, and said, "Linda, don't do this. We have plans to send you up the ladder. This is a union labor relations year, and we already have you slotted to sit at the bargaining tables. We wanted to teach you negotiations. Stay. Your future is bright here."

If I didn't feel miserable enough when I walked in, that did it for sure. Everything in me wanted to scream, "I've changed my mind!" but I had to do what God wanted me to do. I had to take up my cross and follow Him, and that day, I understood just how heavy that cross can be. With eyes cast down and a heavy heart, I told my boss, "I'm so sorry, but I have to do this," and walked out with my thoughts steeled on the new life that lay ahead, determined to leave the other behind.

Once I had completed my final two weeks with the company, I flew to Savannah to meet Brad and start house hunting. Rather than living within the city limits, we chose a new brick home on Wilmington Island, right off the coastline. We returned to Ohio to pack up and headed to our new destination. I did a last walkthrough of our empty little Ohio house and allowed the hot salty tears to slide down my cheeks. Resolutely, I shut the door, signaling the end of that four-year era of our lives. God was completely in charge as we moved toward our cavernous, unknown future.

The Angel of the Lord

Brad's new territory was expansive, which required him to travel two weeks out of every month. The week we moved in, he had to leave on a business trip; and there I was, alone in a strange city, far away from home, not knowing anyone, and being forced to stay overnight by myself. I opened my Bible to Psalm 91 (NIV) and was comforted by this passage:

> He who dwells in the shelter of the Most High,
> will rest in the shadow of the Almighty.
> I will say of the Lord, "He is my refuge and
> my fortress, my God, in whom I trust.
> You will not fear the terror of night...
> For he will command his angels concerning
> you to guard you, in all your ways; they will lift
> you up in their hands...

"God," I prayed, "this is your promise, and there's no one else here to whom I can turn. Please calm my fears and keep me safe."

As I prayed those words, the physical world disappeared, and I had a vision into the spiritual world, the first vision since the one I'd had when I was baptized in the Holy Spirit at age eleven. The Lord allowed me to see His angel stationed on the roof of our house at the front door overhang. The angel was quite large and sat cross-legged, displaying a huge flaming sword held in both hands in front of him. His robe was pure white, and he had brown shoulder-length hair but no facial hair. It was obvious that he was on guard, for his face was fierce.

I was graciously permitted to see that angel in order to settle my fears. It gave me peace, and I eventually drifted off to sleep. From then on, I would read Psalm 91 before I retired each night, trusting that the angel was continually on watch over me. But that wasn't the last time I would see him. I would be granted another glimpse of that angel, which would once again prove God's protection over me.

The second occurrence happened several months after our move, and once again, Brad was out of town. As was my routine, I read Psalm 91, said my prayers, clicked off the light, and dropped off into a deep sleep. Sometime around two o'clock in the morning, I woke up with a jolt, completely lucid, and was petrified at what I beheld. A very discernable, very black outline of what appeared to be a man, though I knew it was not human, stood in the doorway of my bedroom. It had no distinguishable features other than being a dense black shadow. I sensed its malevolence and froze as I stared in horror at the menacing apparition. Perspiration beaded across my forehead, and my breathing came in short blasts. My entire body shook with fear while clutching the edge of the blanket as if it were my shield of protection. And then I heard what turned out to be my own terrified scream, *"Jesus, Jesus! Help me!"*

In a flash of a moment, the angel whom God had assigned to me, flew to the doorway, brandishing his fiery sword, and wrestled the black shadow down to the floor in lethal combat, with the angel being atop the evil one. As I watched in terror, the scene very slowly faded away until there was no trace of the vision, and everything had returned to normal—everything, that is, except me. I was shaken to my very core, but I knew I had experienced the Lord's hand of protection against what I perceived was a demonic presence. From that night on, I knew God would take care of me. Whatever I faced, He would be there. That evil spirit never returned. It was another lesson of God's faithfulness.

We need to understand that we have authority in Christ to cast out evil spirits. His Word says, "I have given you authority to trample on snakes and scorpions and to overcome all the power of the enemy; nothing will harm you" Luke 10:9 (NIV). Darkness has to flee at the name of Jesus! That night proved to me the veracity of His Word.

There were lessons that the Lord wanted to teach me that I would have never learned if He hadn't removed and isolated me from all things familiar. He showed me that He alone was my Source for everything. He allows adversities and challenges to come into our lives to prove that He can be trusted and to demonstrate His power in all circumstances and to grow our faith. I was to learn many of those lessons over the next two years.

What Now?

I exhausted all of the historic tours in and around Savannah, traveled a little with Brad to some of the outlying islands off the

Georgia coast, and then wondered what I was to do with myself from then on. We were already established in a church where I was involved in the music ministry, and I would often go out to lunch with my newfound friends or take a trip to Atlanta to shop. But that got old, and I needed to find something more to do. I would often cry out, "Lord, what am I to do here?"

I eventually signed up with a temporary employment agency just so I'd have something to do and, subsequently was offered a part-time job with a real estate attorney doing title searches. Though I liked that job, it seemed that gone was the big career or any hope of one. I figured that I would not be able to pursue a corporate career anymore as I'd probably have to give it up again anyway.

More of You, Lord

With Brad gone so much and only working a couple of days a week, I still had a lot of open time on my hands, and I believe that was by God's design. Often, to get our undivided attention, He will allow us to be in what is referred to as "the desert place," a place of nothingness and, frequently, a place of the fiery furnace. If you choose to go God's way, surrendering your will to Him and desiring Him to use you for His purposes, then know this—you too will go by way of the desert. It is a part of the spiritual journey where we are stripped of our own desires and are fired in His furnace. All that can be seen is a barren wasteland and little else. But it's the place where He makes us malleable and pliable in His hands so that He can shape us the way He chooses on His potter's wheel. However, take heart; God doesn't leave us there forever, although sometimes it may seem so.

In the classic allegory, *Hind's Feet on High Places*, Hannah Hurnard writes that the Shepherd takes Much-Afraid to the desert, but Much-Afraid views it as abhorrent. She does not want to go there, like most of us. But the Shepherd states that those who are called to High Places must all pass through the desert.

"Much-Afraid," he said, "all of my servants on their way to the High Places have had to make this detour through the desert.

It is called 'The furnace of Egypt, and an horror of great darkness,' (Genesis 15:12, 17). Here they have learned many things which otherwise they would have known nothing about."[3]

The heroes of the Bible had to pass this way, too. There was Moses, who sat in the back side of the desert for forty years; Joseph was a slave and imprisoned thirteen years in Egypt; David was on the run from King Saul in the desert for eight years; Paul spent three years in the desert after his encounter on the Damascus Road; and Jesus also endured a period of fasting and temptation in the desert before beginning His ministry. All of these, and others, had their desert time before being released into their destinies.

Even though I didn't have a name for it then, that's exactly where I was. I spent much of my time in the Word, and it was here I learned to fast, intercede in prayer, and become a worshipper. I was hungry for the things of God and became a God-chaser. God became an insatiable itch that just couldn't be scratched enough. I couldn't get enough of His presence. I couldn't hear from Him enough or talk about Him enough. I desperately wanted Him to use me but didn't know just how. I read every book I could find on the gifts of the Spirit, heavenly encounters, and supernatural interventions. I watched all of the Christian TV programs on TBN, PTL, and CBN. I was seeking Him with all of my heart, soul, mind, and strength, but I didn't see much of anything ahead for my future, and I didn't have a clue where I was headed—if I was headed anywhere at all, for that matter. Frankly, I didn't even think I had a future. I had surrendered everything to God, and all I could see was an empty no man's land. Even though I was making major spiritual strides, I had nothing much to do. I traded in all of my dreams for His, but He didn't seem to have a dream for me. My life appeared devoid of all direction. I decided that God must not have had a destiny for me after all. Maybe I had made it all up in my head.

But I was wrong—dead wrong—because He was about to open the door of a secret dream that I had hidden from everyone. It was

---

[3]   Hannah Hurnard, *Hind's Feet on High Places* (Wheaton, Illinois: Living Books, Tyndale House Publishers) P. 85

only the ears and eyes of God who heard and saw when I would daydream about this in my little lavender-and-white bedroom as I was growing up, and He was about to reveal to me that He knew all about it.

A Model Citizen

As a teenager, I loved reading fashion magazines, particularly *Seventeen Magazine.* The faces of supermodels Cheryl Tiegs and Twiggy would grace the cover pages, and I would envision myself as a model sashaying down the catwalk adorned with the latest designs or smiling from the print work of an advertisement slick or maybe even pitching a product in a television commercial. I didn't need to be a supermodel, but just working as a model sure held a fascination for me. However, I also knew the main requirement—one had to be tall to be a model—and my five-foot-four-inch height wasn't going to cut it. Eventually, I left that fantasy in the dustbin of my mind and let the years sweep it away.

I did get a little taste of it, though, when I worked for an aluminum company one summer. The advertising department asked if I'd pose for a new brochure they were creating. A glamorous photoshoot? You bet! I got all gussied up and reported on the set only to find a bunch of four-foot-high aluminum ingots set around. I was to pose in the midst of about half a dozen of those metal blocks. Glamorous indeed! Somehow, I was to make those ingots look so desirable that the whole industry would want to run out and buy them. I tried all kinds of smiley poses while battling to keep those things standing upright. I leaned on some of the obelisks and some of them leaned on me. So much for the dazzling world of the bold and beautiful! I packed that experience up with a giggle, along with my long-gone daydreams and would never have guessed it would one day resurface.

I continued to ask God what He intended for my life. What was His will? Surely it wasn't just to work a couple of days a week tracing land grants. I'd always been goal-oriented. This waiting period was way off my chart. I was ambitious, and I was growing impatient. Psalm 27:14 (NLT) admonishes us to "Wait patiently for the

Lord, be brave and courageous. Yes, wait patiently for the Lord." We humans don't usually do very well with patience. Don't you wish there was a cell app called "Patience" that you could download and—*poof*—you'd get a surge of patience? But that's not God's way. He gives us "opportunities" to develop our patience through difficult co-workers, tedious family members, freeway traffic jams, and job hunts! And in this case, I was to do the waiting on my knees to allow God to continue to work in my life. And He did.

As I scanned the newspaper one evening, I noticed an announcement that a new modeling agency had opened in town. They were seeking men and women to be trained for fashion shows, print work, film, and trade shows. The ad didn't say anything about height requirements, so, having nothing else to do, I called for an appointment. The owner of the agency was tall, attractive, and had worked as a high-fashion model in New York, Paris, and Germany. Fat chance I had! She asked me some questions about my background and then put me through my paces. She had me walk, read some advertising copy, and then took test shots. I didn't expect all of that nor was I prepared for it. I thought it would just be an interview. I was then thanked and told I'd hear back in a day or so. Chalk that one up to a "thanks but no thanks, Linda," I glumly thought as I left her office.

A day or so later, I got the call. As soon as I heard her German accent, I knew who it was. *Yeah, yeah,* I thought. *Let's get the "thanks but no thanks" over with.*

"Leenda, dees ees Ursula from dee modeling agency. Ve vould like to represent you as model eef you still be interested." Huh? I was really taken aback. Sure, I was still interested!

I was scheduled to start training at the agency a week later. There were a couple of dozen others in the class, and although I was one of the shortest in the group, I learned that not all modeling jobs require sky-walkers. I could work as a petite model in fashion shows and could do commercial print, film, and trade shows. Thus, I began this audacious new career in a whole new industry. Once trained, I did a photo shoot for my portfolio and was then sent on "go sees" (interviews); and lo and behold, I began to get booked for various projects.

My first job was a fashion show at a local restaurant, and then other assignments came along. I was booked for print work and did trade shows at some of the big hotels, and in due course, I got hired for TV commercials. My first commercial was for a clothing store, and one of the things I had to do was ride a bike. After a few shaky practice attempts (I hadn't ridden a bike in years), we were ready to do the shoot on location at a park.

Those commercials ignited a fire of "acting fever" within me, and those former years of California dreamin', marched across my mind once again. I would say to Brad, "Wouldn't it be something if Kellogg's would move us to Los Angeles? Maybe I'd be able to work in Hollywood." I really think God was giving me that dream. There were actually more reasons for the Lord leading me in this direction than just letting me have fun acting in front of a camera. Years later, I would later be able to see what His purposes actually were.

Brad's answer to me was based on corporate history. A typical Kellogg's career path would involve his next-level promotion to a moderate-sized market that had wider exposure and a little more responsibility in areas that his present territory didn't offer. The major metropolitan markets, like Los Angeles, were for those with moderate-market experience, and more often than not, Kellogg's salesmen usually remained within their own sales region and were never transferred all the way across the continent. So even if he was promoted several more times, the likelihood of going to Los Angles was slim to none.

At one point, he was considered for a promotion to Fargo, North Dakota, but didn't get that opportunity. He was really disappointed, but I wasn't. I didn't want to go to freezing Fargo—I wanted to go to lovely Los Angeles! I continued to work at my craft and get as much experience as I could and kept my dream of warm and sunny California alive in my heart.

And then, almost two years from the day that we had moved to Savannah, Brad came home from work all excited. A promotion opportunity was being offered to us again. He didn't know where, but his division manager was to call at seven o'clock that evening to present the package. My mind whirled back to two years earlier when the Lord asked me to surrender all. I was nervous. Again, I had a career going and, again, I would have to leave it behind. How many times would I have to do this? "Yet Lord, I promised I'd go where You wanted me to go. Thy will be done." I sighed. "But I pray that Your will is not Fargo!"

The clock struck seven o'clock that evening, and the phone rang right on schedule. Brad picked it up and the conversation commenced. My heart raced as all kinds of thoughts tumbled through my mind. I stood right next to him with my ear to the phone in hopes of catching where our future would take us next.

Suddenly, Brad's eyes grew really wide. I couldn't hear what was being said.

"Where? Where?" I urgently whispered, and he mouthed, "*Los Angeles, California!*"

I screamed. I jumped up and down for joy like a three-year-old child at a birthday party. I danced. I praised God. And I was beside myself! Brad was trying to quiet me down so he could hear the rest of the conversation. His boss then asked him how I would feel about going to LA. Brad said he'd ask me, covered the phone, and laughingly inquired if I was willing to go to Los Angeles, California. Amidst my tears of joy, I couldn't say "yes" fast enough!

The conversation ended with his boss promising to send details concerning the move.

We were stunned! Brad's supervisors had confidence in his abilities and went to bat for him to move him two positions up to a major market across the entire United States. We found out later that it was an unprecedented corporate move. Brad had the favor of the One greater than any of them. Our Father did it again. Not only did He fulfill the dream in Brad's heart, He also fulfilled the dream in mine!

I couldn't wait to pack up and get on that plane heading west. I decided that I had finally found my God-given destiny. My wildest dream was about to come true. California, here I come!

CHAPTER 7

California, Here I Come!

The day we landed in Los Angeles, I felt as if I was home. It was a warm, sunny day, not a cloud in the sky, with palm trees swaying—all just as I had imagined. I even loved the bustle of the throngs of traffic on the freeways as the car slowly crept out of LAX to our hotel. It seemed that everyone had somewhere exciting to go, and I couldn't wait to have somewhere exciting to go too. Of course, that was until I had to fight the colossal traffic jams myself! But initially, I saw it as all part of the charm of LA.

Brad and I immediately threw ourselves into the business at hand—house hunting. The sooner we found a house, the sooner we could move. I love California, but the housing prices? Eh, not so much! But I was in beautiful California, not far from the beaches that I used to dream about, so that made up for the drawbacks.

We found a little bungalow in the South Bay area and made the move with record speed and then set out to live our California Dream. While Brad's position as metropolitan district manager required a great deal of time, both on the road and in his office, I was trying to decipher how to break into the entertainment industry.

The acting trade papers advertised audition calls, workshops, and photographers, and once I subscribed to those, I was able to get started. I immediately registered for a beginning acting workshop. That really helped get me pointed in the right direction. The acting coach covered techniques on how to audition, the types of photos that casting directors required, the basics of acting, and everything one needed to know to ply the trade. She even worked with us on selecting an a.k.a. (also known as), i.e., a stage name.

Now I was ready to try out my auditioning skills in the big leagues. With my Thomas Guide (a book of local maps) in hand, I slid into the daunting freeway traffic and made my way north to the Hollywood area. My first audition call was for a modeling job. A new designer had made an audition call for women for an ongoing weekly fashion show at an upscale restaurant in Century City. With fear and trembling and lots of "Jesus-help-mes," I entered a tiny upstairs showroom located in a dingy warehouse that was cluttered with bolts of fabric and bits of trim and mannequins draped with the designer's latest fashion ideas. Not glamorous by any means, but I would eventually realize that this was the norm. The designer looked over my resume, asked to see my portfolio, had me demonstrate my runway walk, and hired me on the spot! Thus, I was launched into my new Hollywood career in "the biz" (show business).

Every Friday, I would sign in at the restaurant along with a couple of other models, and we would whirl and twirl from one table to the next as we showed off the outfits selected for the day. It was a yuppie hangout of sorts, and several of the Hollywood elite would lunch there.

That job was my bread and butter, but what I really wanted was to break into films. I was given a tip by an industry insider that a great way to learn and be "seen" was to sign up as an atmosphere person...a nice way of describing an extra. Extras are the actors in films who make up the crowds or additional people on the streets, etc. So I watched the trades and answered calls for film extras. Often, I would get picked out of the extras crowd for bit parts (small standout parts). First, it started as separate walk-ons (chosen apart from the extras crowd to appear separately on camera) or silent bits (non-speaking acting roles that are a little more than a walk-on); then, I graduated into small roles. Sometimes, those roles would end up on the cutting room floor (edited out of the film), but at other times, my scenes were left in the movie. Regardless, it was a great way to learn and make connections.

***

The first big goal of all beginning actors is to get into an acting union, such as the Screen Actors Guild (SAG) or American Film, Television, and Radio Artists (AFTRA). SAG is the coveted union where all screen actors strive to become members. Being a union member separates the neophytes from the professionals and puts one on the union pay scale. The prerequisite criterion for joining SAG is to land a speaking role. It's a real Catch-22, however, because in order to get a speaking role in a movie, one first has to be a union member; but to become a union member, one first has to be offered a speaking role in a film. It was the dilemma that all of us newbies would discuss and scratch our heads over as to how to make that happen. Then, on one film project, I finally caught a break.

I had answered the call for extras on a feature film. The second assistant director, better known as the second AD, gave the extras group some direction, and we did our little crowd scene. The second AD is the one to impress at this level, and I must have done something right because everyone was thanked and dismissed except me. He took me aside and asked if I had my SAG card yet—or in other words, was I a union member. My heart beat fast.

"No," I answered hopefully.

Then he said the magic words. "Well, we're going to make sure you get it." With that, he went to the film's director, had a speaking role written in for me, and just like that, I qualified for my SAG card. Eventually, I was able to gain membership in AFTRA as well. As the psalmist puts it in Psalm 84:11b (KJV), "No good thing will he withhold from them that walk uprightly."

This gentleman never asked for anything in return. He knew I was a Christian as I had at one point had the opportunity to witness to him about Jesus. He didn't seem to quite understand, but I told him anyway.

But there is definitely a seedy side to Hollywood. Although my mission was always to share the Good News wherever I went and try to stay away from everything unseemly, one evening, I got a good dose of the dark side of Hollywood that was not only a shock but a heartbreaker.

After the completion of that film, I was invited to the wrap party, the celebration that occurs when the filming of a project is finished. It was my first wrap party, and of course, I looked forward to it. It was held at the film director's home, high in the Hollywood Hills. I was so excited to have an invitation to attend. Brad and I set out for our new adventure, all bright-eyed and bushy-tailed, never dreaming that we would encounter a part of Hollywood that would absolutely stun us. The house was at the pinnacle of one of the hills and commanded a magnificent view overlooking the city. Because the party was so well attended, we had to park our car on the street about a half a mile down the hill and walk up to the house. My new friend, the second AD, welcomed us at the door. We were taking in the beauty of the house when he offered to show us around. That's when things began to go sideways.

He led us down a hall into a side room, stating, "This is the cocaine room, if you're into crack." The room was dark except for a small lamp in the corner. People were lying on sofas and draped across chairs, completely maxed out. He nonchalantly shut the door and proceeded to an adjacent room. "If opium is your pleasure, this is the room where you can get it." Again, people were strung out across furniture or lying on the floor of the dimly lit room. He quietly shut that door and headed down a flight of stairs. "Now down here, we have laughing gas if you prefer." By then, Brad and I were giving each other sidelong looks, absolutely dumbfounded at the misguided souls before us. We headed back up the stairway and were asked if we wanted to try the marijuana room, at which point we hurriedly said, "We'd just like a soda, thanks."

When our host disappeared into the kitchen to fetch our beverage of choice, Brad whispered, "Make your rounds, and let's get out of here." I couldn't agree more. Not only was this naïve, small-town, Christian girl in shock, but I was disconsolate for these people who lived their lives in such a dark, vile place without knowing how much Jesus loved them.

After we politely drank our sodas, we made my rounds to the director and all of the appropriate movers and shakers, and then quietly slipped out the door and ran down the hill to our car like two dragsters racing toward the finish line. I felt as though we were at the gates of hell and was nauseated and overwhelmed by the memory of the appalling things I had seen—a sad pictorial of the underpinnings of the movie industry. Up to that point, the Lord had protected me from all of that evil, but that night, He allowed me to see the hidden underworld. I began to pray more earnestly that His power would invade Hollywood.

***

It wasn't until about three years into the acting that I was offered the lead role in an independent feature film. Up to that point, I had only gotten small bit roles, so this was a big deal to me. I got the call one morning after having gone to that audition and a couple of call-backs the week before. Granted, it was a low-budget film, but that's often how acting careers progress. The casting director presented the terms over the telephone, and I told him I'd have my agent call him. At the very end of the conversation, he stated one *tiny* detail that he had failed to mention previously. There was one scene that required some "minimal" nudity—something that, by Hollywood standards, was no big deal, but by my Christian standards, it certainly was! Had I known about this at the auditions, I would have walked away. However, when auditioning, you only get what are called "sides," a section of the script that contains just a scene or sometimes only one page of a scene. I hadn't been given the whole script as yet. Unless you are an A-list star, rarely do you get the entire script ahead of time for an audition.

I had worked for years to finally get to this point. Now I had a decision to make: do I walk away from everything I worked so hard for or compromise everything I stood for? Surrendering to God is ongoing because life is ongoing. It's not just a one-shot, and then we never have to deal with it again. I was at another crossroads, but it didn't take me but a split second to give an answer.

"Mr. ——," I said, "I appreciate the offer, and I'm really flattered that you've chosen me for this project, but I'm a Christian, and I can't compromise myself to do this. So thank you, but I have to decline the role."

He was quiet for a moment. Then he tried to talk me into it, but I held my ground, thanked him, and hung up. I was completely bummed. After all of those years of work, it came down to this? There will always be temptations no matter what field of work we are in. Satan is always laying traps for us. We need to constantly be on alert.

Amazingly, the next morning I got a call from that casting director again. He had a counter-offer for me from the director. That rarely ever happens! He tried to negotiate with me again. I wouldn't have to do that scene, he said. The role was being re-written so that a different character would do that part. Now I was on the hot seat again. Could I allow myself to even be associated with a project like that even if I wasn't the one acting it out? Satan's trap was set again.

"Surely," the devil whispered, "the Lord will overlook that little compromise. After all, you've worked so hard to get to this point, and you won't be the one to do that scene. And this could be the beginning of something big!" The devil is cunning. He will relentlessly twist and turn things so that sin looks acceptable and exciting. He will try to deceive us by asking, "What's the big deal?" But don't do it! One compromise will lead to another until the line becomes blurred. Compromise is a way of desensitizing our morals and whittling down our principals. In 1 Peter 5:8–9 (NIV), we are warned, "Be self-controlled and alert. Your enemy the devil prowls around like a roaring lion looking for someone to devour. Resist him standing firm in the faith, because you know that the family of believers throughout the world is undergoing the same kind of sufferings."

I sighed, "No, Mr. ——, as a Christian, I just can't be a part of that."

His answer surprised me. "I have to admit, I have a lot of respect for you," he said. "Most would jump at the chance. I wish you the best." That ended the conversation, and I never heard from him again.

Though the projects that I was blessed enough to work on all sound very glowing and thrilling, there were plenty, and I mean plenty, more rejections and disappointments than roles. The statistics are that for every one hundred auditions, you might land one job. Not great odds, and having had the experience, I believe those numbers to be true. The competition is fierce with talented people literally from all over the world coming to Hollywood to make it in entertainment. It takes a great deal of stamina, persistence, and thick skin to weather through that industry, and for a Christian, sidestepping the compromising pitfalls are a challenge. I would advise any Christian who wants to go into that business to be strong in the faith and always be prayed up. The temptations are great, and it's easy to get caught up in the sweeping desire for fame and fortune at the expense of one's moral compass—even one's soul.

The acting was a journey that the Lord led me through, but in all honesty, it just never really felt like it was my destination. In the back of my head, I somehow just knew that that was not where I was to ultimately be. However, it was one of the ways God used to help me gain confidence and give me the ability to get in front of others. He was training me for my future ministry and the television show that I would later host.

I think too that it was another fulfillment of one of my childhood dreams. Don't ever be afraid to dream. Dream often and dream outrageously. God is watching and listening! Or maybe He's the One who planted it in your heart in the first place...

The Holy Spirit Comes Calling

During the years I was involved in entertainment, the Holy Spirit continued to work in my spiritual life. Because I desperately needed His guidance and protection, I spent a lot of time in the Word and in prayer seeking Him. It's interesting that when we want something badly enough, we will spend that time before Him in prayer so that He will grant us our heart's desire. It's one of the ways He woos us to Himself. He will use all types of situations to get our attention and at that time in my life, He used the acting.

As a result of the amount of time I spent with God, He opened another door to something I earnestly sought—to be used in the operation of the supernatural gifts of the Spirit as outlined in 1

Corinthians 12. The Lord saw my heart and sent me someone to encourage and teach me about the work of the Spirit.

A gentleman by the name of Mickey Wagenman was hired to be the principal of our church's Christian school. His wife Carolyn—better known as Cookie—and I became fast friends. Cookie was savvy about the Charismatic Movement and operated in the gifts of the Spirit, predominately in prophecy. Often, she would be invited to speak at women's ministries groups and would minister in the gifts. Although she didn't realize it, and nor did I at the time, she was mentoring me. She was a little older than I, and I think I padded after her like a puppy, watching and learning and asking questions. One of the things that I truly admired about her was that she was fiercely courageous in her walk with the Lord. If He gave her a word, she was bold to proclaim it. I wanted God to use me as He did her.

I'm a huge proponent of mentoring. Elijah mentored Elisha, Paul mentored Timothy, Jesus mentored His disciples who, in turn, mentored the new Christians, and so it continues today. It worked in my life, and I've mentored many others, both knowingly and sometimes unknowingly. The Lord often brings individuals into our lives to serve as pictures for us to observe and often to create a spiritual hunger in our hearts for the work He has in mind for us to do. Cookie was definitely that picture for me. She's still out there in ministry for Jesus and is a great example of being faithful to the call of God on one's life.

It was during that timeframe that God tested me to see if I really meant what I said about the desire to be used by Him. To be His vessel means we have to be obedient and often have to be bold risk-takers. Sometimes He will ask us to do things that seem rather bizarre, but if you notice in many of the accounts in the Bible, God asked a lot of folks to do some pretty strange things. Check out Hosea, whom God told to marry a prostitute; or Gideon, who was told to fight a battle by breaking jars and blowing trumpets; or how about Ezekiel, who lay on his left side for 390 days and then on his right side for 40 days, tied up in ropes as he prophesied. Now I'm not saying to do as they have done by any means! However, God's thoughts are not our thoughts and His ways are higher than ours, and He looks for those who will be obedient to do His bidding.

Since I continually asked the Lord to use me for His glory, He had a little job for me to do. It was a test. Did I really want to be used by God, and would I really be obedient to do as He asked? One morning, I had stopped to get a doughnut at a little shop near our house. As I entered the shop, God highlighted a man to me who stood at the back of the ordering line. I proceeded to the glass counter to check out my pastry options when I heard God speak in that still small voice. "Tell that man I love him, and I want him to know me." This man was a complete stranger, and I couldn't comprehend why in the world God would want me to approach him. But I heard it again. "Tell that man I love him, and I want him to know me."

I argued with the Lord in my spirit but then decided to put it back on Him. "OK, Lord, if you have really spoken to me to do this, then empty the shop out and I'll tell him." I admit I was being a little smug and didn't actually believe that that would happen, because there was a good-sized crowd in there. However, no sooner had it left my thoughts than the people began to disperse until only the two of us were left in the shop. Even the cashier had to excuse herself and went to the back room. At that point, I got nervous, worried about what he might say and laugh all the way out the door. Now my pride was at stake. You see, God's not out to wound our pride, He's out to kill it, and mine needed a bullet that day! Being obedient and bold has everything to do with getting rid of our pride to do His will. My spirit fought it, but finally, I gave my pride a good death stab. We can't ask God to use us, and then, when He gives us opportunity, run away and tell Him, "I was just kidding."

I took a deep breath, turned toward the man, and said in a squeaky voice, "Sir, I don't know if you will understand this, but God told me to tell you that He loves you, and He wants you to know him." I swallowed hard and waited for the big hee-haw. But he didn't laugh.

He stared at me for a few seconds and then asked, "What did you say?"

Oh great! Now I had to repeat it! I took a deep breath and said it again.

He stared hard at me. "Why did you say that?" he quizzed. By that time, I had wilted inside. This wasn't going quite as I had hoped.

My brilliant answer was a very tenuous "Because God told me?" I was ready to rush out the door but was saved by the cashier, who miraculously appeared from the back to take our orders.

After I got my pastries, I speedily headed toward the door, but the gentleman said to me, "Wait a minute. I want to talk to you."

We left the shop together. As we walked out into the wide span of the parking lot, he turned to me and commented, "My son believes like you. This morning, he called to invite me to some revival meeting they were having tonight at his church. He's been after me to go to church with him for a long time. I initially told him no, but now that you said what you did, I've changed my mind. I'm going to go. Do you think God really does love me?"

I answered that, without a doubt, God loved him and wanted a relationship with him. He intently listened as I shared more on God's love for us through His Son Jesus, and then we parted ways. I never saw that man again, but my prayer is that he went to that revival meeting and gave his life to the Lord who was in pursuit of him.

That little episode catapulted my faith, and I earnestly began to listen for more of God's instructions. I was elated to know I had heard the voice of God and made a difference in someone's life. I wanted more experiences like that and rushed home to call Cookie to report my story.

***

I continued to grow spiritually and sincerely listened for God's voice. I wanted more experiences with Him. I wanted to do His will. One thing about our Savior is that if we mean it, He will answer and surprise us with opportunities that we could never predict. Luke 11:10 (NIV) states clearly that "For everyone who asks receives; the one who seeks finds; and to the one who knocks, the door will be opened."

The Father had another one of those surprise moments await-ing me. One Sunday morning in that same year, our pastor's wife approached me after service and asked if she could talk with me pri-vately. Curious, I followed her to a corner of the vestibule. She stated that she had decided to step down from the leadership of our wom-en's ministries and felt that the Lord was telling her that I was to be the next president. Man, I didn't see that one coming!

For the preceding year, I had been on the women's ministry board and led the praise and worship during the meetings, but I had no aspirations to take on the leadership. No way! Not quite into my thirties, I was one of the youngest members of the group. Why would all of those older women want to listen to me? But even more than that, I had the fear of speaking in front of others. I could sing all day but…ugh…don't ask me to speak! I gave her all of the why-not excuses, but she would not be deterred. Finally, she patted my hand and said, "You just pray about it." OK, I thought, I'll pray about it, but you've got it wrong. I'm sure the Lord will say the same thing that I'm saying. "No, not her!"

A couple of days later, I figured I had better pray about it, if only to tell the pastor's wife that I had. I got onto my knees by my bed and prayed something like, "Lord, You and I both know that I'm not the right person to take over the leadership of women's ministries. You and I both know I'm too young and no one is going to listen to me, not to mention that I'm too frightened to talk in front of others. So since we both agree on all of the above, I will tell the pastor's wife 'no' and that she got it wrong. In Jesus's name I pray, Amen." I let out a sigh of relief. It was all settled. I got off my knees and sat on the bed.

I hadn't had my devotions for the day as yet, so I shot up a quick prayer asking the Lord what He wanted me to read that day, and I randomly opened my Bible. It flipped to Jeremiah 1, and my eyes fell on verse 4 (TLB), "The Lord said to me, 'I knew you before you were formed within your mother's womb; before you were born I sanctified you and appointed you as my spokesman to the world.' 'Oh Lord God,' I said, 'I can't do that! I'm far too young! I'm only a youth!' 'Don't say that,' he replied, 'for you will go wherever I send you and speak whatever I tell you to. And don't be afraid of the people, for I, the Lord, will be with you and see you through.' "

I was incredulous! I blinked hard a couple of times and read it again. It jumped out at me like a Las Vegas billboard, and I knew exactly what it meant—God was telling me to take on women's ministries. "Too young" was not an option with Him, and "too scared" wouldn't cut it either. There was no way I could get around it. If I wanted to follow Jesus, I couldn't pick and choose what I would and wouldn't do. The Holy Spirit's leading is not a menu. I had tried to wrestle with it and spin it to mean something else, but in the end, I lost the battle. There was nothing left to do but pick up the phone and call the pastor's wife with a "yes" answer, but of course, she already knew.

I didn't have a clue what to do when I took the women's ministries leadership over, but the Lord was with me and made up for my incompetence. We planned a lot of fun and creative programs and had some amazing speakers. I leaned on God to direct me, step by step. This ministry was more training ground for what God was calling me to do. God had a plan, and all I had to do was obediently follow Him.

***

I was twenty-nine years old when the Lord first used me in the gift of tongues during a Sunday morning church service. An unusually heavy anointing swept through the congregation. I had my hands raised and was enjoying the presence of the Lord like everyone else. Suddenly, I felt the weight of His glory come over me and an urge to speak out in my heavenly prayer language. To be completely transparent with my readers, I must admit, I was so scared that I tried to quench it. We are told not to quench the Spirit (1 Thessalonians 5:19), but I am forthcoming when I tell you that I tried. I began to cry and shake, overcome with His power. I grabbed the pew in front of me to steady myself but, instead, caused the pew to shake as well. Brad grabbed my hand on the pew to try to settle me, but he began to shake with me. Those who stood in front of that pew turned around to see what was going on. We were quite a spectacle, I fear. The presence of God was so strong that I finally went with it and burst out with a of blast tongues.

I felt a lot better and was excited about my new gift when it dawned on me…the associate pastor and his wife were out of town, and they were the only ones in the church who had the gift of interpretation. Oh no! My first message in tongues and no one to interpret it! I knew the instructions given in 1 Corinthians 14 that, if there's no one to interpret the unknown language in a corporate setting, we are to be silent and not give it or we are to ask for and give the interpretation ourselves. I wasn't going to ask for the interpretation—I barely had the faith to give the message in tongues, and I couldn't take the tongues back! I went back into panic mode. What will the congregation and all of my friends think? What will the pastor think?

Then, like a trumpet blast, I heard an unfamiliar voice from the platform begin to interpret. I later learned it was the visiting missionary who was to give the morning message. I felt a vast relief followed by great joy. Thank you, Jesus! What a thrill!

As time passed, the Lord gifted me with the ability to interpret messages in tongues and then moved me on to deliver prophecies, both corporately and personally. Those came easier once I really began to recognize the voice of God.

Back to Business

The time arrived when it became clear to me that God was closing the doors to the acting. I had mixed emotions about relinquishing that part of my life. I was tired of the constant drives to Hollywood/LA, and the endless auditioning and the considerable amounts of money needed for all of the expenses involved, with only a fraction of return from my investment. And there were an increasing number of acting projects I couldn't attach my name to because of the worldly slant. Yet I had put a huge amount of time and money into my acting, and I hated to just walk away. But the doors slammed tightly shut, and there was no use beating on them. I perceived that season was over for me, and I knew it was time to go. When God says it's time, it's time. White-knuckling something will only cause frustration. Our lives are in seasons. "There is a time for everything; and a season for every activity under heaven" Ecclesiastes 3:1 (NIV). That season had come to an end.

Not knowing what else to do, I returned to the business world. Tenuously, I put my resume back on the street and was hired fairly quickly by a cutting-edge technology company located at the old Gower Studios (formerly Columbia Pictures Studios) on Sunset Boulevard in Hollywood. It was a start-up company established by a couple of technology geeks with an ahead-of-their-time vision. I was brought in to help hire the office staff, establish company policy, purchase office furniture and equipment, and perform an untold myriad of tasks to help get the company up and running.

In less than a year, the company had outgrown its location, and new digs were needed. Instead of leasing the usual high-rise office space, we leased a turn-of-the-century Queen Anne mansion in Hancock Park. The mansion had been used as a location for filming several TV shows and movies, one of them being the 1971 thriller *Willard*. It was great fun working there, and once I got over my acting disappointments and released it all to the Lord, I truly enjoyed my job. On occasion, I would travel on company business, particularly to the Silicon Valley. This was the early 1980s, and I even had a computer in my house with email long before most people ever knew what a PC was.

Now I had a full-time job with a full-time paycheck—that part I liked. Once the company was finally established, I received promotions and pay increases, and it seemed to be the perfect time for Brad and me to purchase a new home. But where? Cookie told us about a church where her sister attended, Christian Chapel of Walnut, and suggested we visit the church, and if we liked it, perhaps we could consider living in that area. We checked it out on the map and saw it was within driving distance of both of our jobs; so one Sunday morning, we decided to take Cookie's advice and visited the church. We fell in love with it! It was an independent Charismatic church with a large congregation. That morning, we were able to meet Senior Pastor Jesse Mason and his wife, Clare, who had been missionaries to

China prior to pastoring there. We visited a few more Sundays and felt that that's where the Lord wanted us to be. We started our search for a home nearby, settling on a new housing development a few miles away. Maybe that's the best idea when house hunting—find a church first instead of the other way around!

After much prayer for God's will and direction, everything seemed to point to "go." We left our little South Bay bungalow behind and eagerly transported ourselves into our newly built home. Life was good and the future looked bright—or was it?

CHAPTER 8

The School of the Holy Ghost

How could this have happened? I fumed to myself as I left work that day. *Everything was going so well. How could they have missed this?* I pulled out of the company-leased parking garage situated catty-corner from our unorthodox offices. I tried to wrap my brain around what had been relayed to me earlier that day.

I nosed my car east and tried to pay attention to the rush-hour traffic, but my thoughts were far away. I mulled over the previous several months during which I was transferred from office manager to sales representative. The new position required nationwide travel to trade shows and conventions to educate the related industries and public about our new service that would soon be introduced into the marketplace. It was an exciting marriage of electronics and cable television, and we were the leaders in the field. To me, it was a dream job and often included press interviews and TV news features. I had just returned from one such trade show the week before in San Antonio, Texas, and I was fired up. We had some potential customers lined up who were extremely interested in the service as soon as it was released. The newly manufactured hardware was sitting on the docks in Japan, awaiting shipment...and now this!

I relived the conversation in my mind that I had with the company president that morning. His tone was grave. "Linda, we have to hold up the deals with the cable companies for now. Unfortunately, we have run out of funds and have to stop all negotiations until we can find new investors to help us with the hardware shipment. As a matter of fact, we are going to have to start employee layoffs." His voice was measured, but I could tell by his body language that he was worried. Evidently, research and development went way beyond what was originally budgeted, and a great deal more funding was needed to bring it all to fruition.

Alarmed, I looked at my immediate supervisor, who was also sitting in on the meeting. He looked as helpless as I felt and just shrugged his shoulders. There was nothing he could add.

An open letter went out later that afternoon to all the employees, and the sad state of affairs was disclosed. The mood was somber as we left our offices at the end of the day. As I negotiated the congested freeways, all I could think about was that I was in jeopardy of losing another dream job, and that Brad and I would be unable to pay our large mortgage and the mountain of expenses that accompanied the purchase of a brand-new home. We needed my salary, and this situation felt eerily reminiscent of my Ohio days.

"How are you going to fix this one, Father God?" I mused.

The weeks progressed, and as promised, several employees were laid off. I knew that if the company did not receive an injection of cash very soon, I too would be gone, and unfortunately, it came to pass. Though I was one of the last to exit the company, that day did eventually arrive. The immense front doors of the beautiful mansion-office were closed for the last time, and so died the new and awe-inspiring technological idea that we had all thrown our talents behind. It was another trial, another disappointment with which to deal, and another closed door.

I signed up for unemployment benefits and was eligible to receive payments for the following eight months, but all I could think of was that I urgently needed to find another job. My unemployment check wasn't enough to cover all of the expenses we had incurred; it certainly didn't look like it on paper when we had budgeted it out, but strangely, somehow it sufficed. In those days, we literally experienced the miracle of the five loaves and two fish. It was a great lesson in God's faithfulness, learning to lean on Him for provision one day at a time. We learned to walk by faith and not by sight, for my life was about to take a dramatic turn, and I would need to learn how to appropriate that faith.

I updated my resume and set out to find a new job, but no matter what I did, no matter how many interviews I went on, and no matter how much I prayed, it seemed like "the heavens were as brass." Two months later, while in prayer, I asked God why He hadn't opened an employment door for me. I finally got my answer, but it wasn't the answer I would have imagined.

His voice was distinct, and there was no doubt that God had spoken. "I am putting you in the school of the Holy Ghost," He said. "I am calling you to prayer, to the Word, and to holiness." And that was it. I knew that no job would be forthcoming. God wanted time with me. I was in training for the ministry, although I didn't quite know what that ministry was as yet, but I had a sense that I was being called. I would have to trust Him to provide for our financial needs in the meantime.

I spent the summer and autumn in God's presence on my knees, fasting, and reading the Word. He took me to that secret place, a place of intimacy where I was shut in with only Him. Sometimes He would speak to me, and there were times that I would have revelatory dreams. It was an amazing season and a paradigm shift in my life that would move me into a whole new arena.

The Call

It was in the fall of that year that I finally received the layout of my ministry from the Lord. It was on the morning of the twenty-ninth of October 1984. The days were mild, with only a hint of crisp air in the evenings to indicate a season change was on its way, and my spiritual season was about to change as well. It was a regular Monday morning, with no indication that anything out of the ordinary was lying in wait out in the wings of my life. I poured myself a cup of coffee, grabbed my Bible for my daily devotions, and settled on the familiar green-plaid family room sofa. It was my favorite place and time of day when I was home alone with no distractions except the monotonous tick of the wall clock. I would read the Word, write in my journal, and worship God.

This time, however, as I sat with pen poised over my journal page, I suddenly had a vision. I drew on a blank sheet what I saw in the spirit realm. It was an umbrella with eight ribs. Hanging down from each rib was a string with a tag attached. The tags named different gifts and areas of ministry. The Lord impressed on me that the umbrella represented my entire ministry call and the tags were different facets of it. He went on to say that it would be an end-time ministry. For years, I just called it the "Umbrella" for lack of any other name. However, in 2005, I had a dream in which God gave me the name of this ministry: It's Beginning to Rain Ministries. It all rather tied in together with the rain and umbrella theme. It wouldn't be until 2014 that I would officially organize it though. I have, however, seen most of the individual facets of the Umbrella vision come to pass over the years, while a few are yet to be fulfilled.

Immediately, through no effort of my own, the doors began to supernaturally swing open to speak at various groups and churches. "Speaking" was one of the Umbrella tags. When God says something, it will be done as He has said. He promises that He is watching over His Word to assure it is fulfilled.

But I'm getting a little ahead of my story.

He Gives the Desires of the Heart

There were two gifts for which I sought the Lord—the gift of the word of knowledge in conjunction with the gifts of healing. I greatly wanted those gifts. In my dad's latter years of ministry, he operated in those gifts, and I long desired to do so too. Those were the gifts that caught my attention as a child attending the healing revival meetings with my parents. I was still fascinated by them. The interesting thing is that God utilized my dad to get me started in those gifts, and it was in a rather unusual way.

Every Saturday, I would call my parents, who still lived in Pennsylvania. On this one particular Saturday morning, as I had a conversation with my mom, my dad said that the Spirit of the Lord was upon him and needed to talk to me. Mom handed him the phone, and he relayed that he had a word of knowledge that, during our church service the next day, there would be at least three people there who would have inner ear infections. He saw that their ears were draining, and they were in a lot of pain, and the Lord wanted to heal them.

I asked him, "So what I am I supposed to do with that?"

"Just tell your pastor," he said. "He'll know what to do."

That made me a little nervous, but the next morning, I obediently went to Pastor Jesse and told him of the incident. He said to me, "Let's pray about it together." At the end of the prayer in a matter-of-fact tone, he stated, "I feel you should give the word." I hadn't bargained for that! What if Dad didn't get it right? After all, he was 2,300 miles away! Anyway, Brad and I had only been attending that church a few months, and I didn't want to look ridiculous in front of the entire church! I tried to get out of it and push it on to Pastor Jesse, but he would have none of it and walked away.

I was a wreck throughout praise and worship and kept praying that the Lord would do something to get me off the hook. He was about to do something all right and kept whispering to me to trust Him. As the service progressed, the Holy Spirit began to move, and the anointing was heavy. I was on the platform in the choir loft when the praise came to a great crescendo, and at that point, Pastor Jesse announced that I had a word of knowledge. There was nothing I could do but advance toward the pulpit. My legs and hands literally shook as Pastor Jesse passed me the microphone. He put his arm around my shoulders, like a protective father, to help steady and validate me, for which I'll always be grateful, and said, "Now share the word of the Lord with the people." In a barely perceptive, shaky voice, I shared the word of knowledge given to me through my dad and waited…but *no one* moved. In dread, I stared back at the multitude of eyes that peered back at me. At that moment, I understood exactly what Job meant when he said, "What I feared has come upon me; what I dreaded has happened to me" (Job 3:25, NIV).

Pastor Jesse urged that whoever that was needed to come forward. I bowed my head and prayed that the earth would open up and swallow me or that the rapture would take place and take me out at that moment so I could disappear! Of course, neither happened;

however, as I peeked up from my bowed head, to my great relief and joy, there came not three but four people down the aisle. Pastor Jesse then asked that I pray a prayer of healing—and all four of them were immediately healed! (They each attested to it after the prayer.)

Now I was excited, and I wanted to do that again! And sure enough, a couple of weeks later on my way to Sunday morning service, the Holy Spirit spoke to me directly that He was sending a "healing wave" for backs. I was to tell the people that God would heal them of back problems if they would step out into the aisles and take it by faith. I greatly longed to do that but got cold feet during the first service and didn't obey. When I sat down after worship, the Lord spoke to me again and said something that profoundly changed my whole mindset and understanding. He said, "If you want the ministry that I have for you, you have to cooperate with me and act on what I tell you to do. We work as a team."

In 1 Corinthians 3:9 (KJV), we find that "we are labourers together with God." He does His part, but we have our part to do as well. Here, He opened the door for me to do the very thing that I had entreated Him to do, and then I ran away out of fear. But "God has not given us a spirit of fear and timidity, but of power" (2 Timothy 1:7, NLT), and I realized that day that, if I wanted this kind of ministry, then I had to be the one to push past my fear and be a bold risk-taker for the Kingdom, no matter what others said or thought. It was a huge foundational lesson for me, and at that moment, I resolved that I would give that word during the second service, regardless of how frightened I might be, and do anything else my Lord asked me to do. It was a turning point.

As the second service got under way, I felt the anointing of God on me, and at an opportune time, I went to the pulpit and whispered to the pastor what the Lord had said. He handed me the mic, and though I have to admit I was still a little fearful, I took courage and spoke out the word. The people didn't hesitate this time but streamed out into the aisles and altar area en masse. I prayed the prayer of faith, and the crowd began to move in ways they hadn't been able to before. Some bent over, others raised their arms over their heads, and there were those who twisted from side to side. The Holy Spirit showed up in power just as He promised. And so it was that God began to use me in the gift of the word of knowledge and the gifts of healing. Sometimes I would minister from the platform, and other times, it was one-on-one, but to be sure, I was changed forever.

Open Doors

The holidays arrived with sunshine and clear skies—a far cry from our back east winters. My parents came to visit us over Christmas, and I had invited Pastor Jesse and Clare to dinner so they could meet my folks and the man who'd had the word of knowledge for the ear healings a couple of months earlier. That evening, to my surprise, Clare asked if I would teach a four-part series on the gifts of the Holy Spirit in the women's ministries group at the church after the first of the year. It was the beginning of the Umbrella ministry that the Lord had declared only two months prior. I had never spoken on spiritual gifts in front of a group before, but I was willing to share what I had learned and just trust the Holy Spirit for the rest.

Week after week, I sought His lead on each message outline, and week after week, He gave what I needed to impart. The series that I teach today, "Targeting Your Spiritual Gifts," still has much of the same core outline that the Holy Spirit inspired all those years ago. Along with the teaching, the Holy Spirit showed up in a powerful way with healings, prophetic words, and the baptism in the Holy Spirit. God made up for the gaps in my abilities as He showed up every week and showed off His glory.

What I didn't realize in totality at the time was that this was the onset of the fulfillment of the ministry and destiny to which God had called me. I simply thought that Sister Clare just needed a guest speaker for that month; however, as time went on and more speaking opportunities were presented to me, I started to see the pattern.

Right after that four-week series, I got a call from a lady I had met at an Aglow International meeting, a Christian women's fellowship. She and her husband had a little house church established in a neighboring town and asked if I would be a guest speaker at one of their services. She then invited me to speak again a couple of weeks later, and doors continued to open. Now the dots connected. This is what the Lord had prepared me for, and this was why He needed my focus and complete attention those last several months to equip and prepare me. The young girl who wouldn't sing "I'll Go Where You Want Me to Go" many years earlier and who never wanted to be in ministry of any sort now shouted like the prophet Isaiah, "Here I am, Lord! Send me!" I'm sure the Father had a good giggle out of that one. And no, I wasn't called to be a preachers' wife either—I was called to be the preacher! He does have a great sense of humor!

Oh No! Not Again

As far as I was concerned, everything in my life was now in order. I was excited about the things the Lord was doing, and His promises were being fulfilled at rapid speed. And then it happened again…

Brad came home from work one day with that "look" on his face that I now recognized. I cut right to the chase. "Please, don't tell me…" My voice trailed off.

Before we had moved into our new home, Brad had a long conversation with his immediate supervisor, and he was assured there were no promotions in the works for him. As a matter of fact, Brad had basically withdrawn his name for promotion consideration. We were both happy living in Southern California and felt it was God's gift to us to be able to live there. But somewhere, there was a disconnect, and now Brad was offered a promotion as director of division sales in the Midwest. Not only was it another step up, but he would be the youngest to have ever been promoted to this position in the history of the company. Again, an unprecedented move by an unprecedented God!

I felt torn—happy for my husband, not so happy for me. "*But why now, Lord?*" I cried. "*My ministry has just begun to break out here.*" (As if He didn't know, right?) "*And anyway, I don't want to leave California!*" I continued to lament.

It was another test of my will versus His. I was reminded of the commitment I had made in Ohio, and as much as I wanted to stay in my beloved California, once more, I had to pray, "Nevertheless, Thy will be done." So through my tears, I again laid down all of my will, my dreams, and yes, even my ministry before God; and when I did, He gave me a promise from Psalm 126:5–6 (TLB), "Those who sow tears shall reap joy. Yes, they go out weeping, carrying seed for sowing, and return singing, carrying their sheaves."

The word "return" caught my eye, and the Lord spoke, "If you will go as I have set forth for you to do, I will bring you back." Now, I really had to take that by faith, because in reality, Kellogg's never sent any of their promotable people back to any place they had already been. The company wanted to make sure they were exposed to all of the different markets in the country. So if that really did happen, it could only happen by the work of God's hands; regardless, however, I had to choose to follow the Lord's lead whether we returned or not.

Though we had only lived in our new home for ten months, I spiritually grew by huge leaps and bounds. The Word of God says that we are to give honor to whom honor is due, and I believe that I made many of those strides because Pastor Jesse and Clare allowed me to take risks and spread my wings at the church. Pastor Jesse always encouraged me and opened his pulpit up to me. Neither he nor Clare ever felt threatened or jealous but were humble and supportive and helped foster my gifts in order to expand in my calling. They too were mentors in my life. It is important that we are allowed to have what I call "spiritual playpens" where we can feel safe to learn and train and make mistakes so that we can fulfill the dreams and destiny that God has placed in our hearts.

Unfortunately, not everyone takes that stance, and rather than encourage the growth of others, some try to be dream killers, afraid that others might get ahead of them. Jill Austin puts this very aptly in her book, *Dancing With Destiny*. She states, "If people have vision for their lives and stick their heads up to pursue something significant, then they are criticized for being proud. In fact, those who do stand out will be taught a lesson in humility by having their heads cut off so they remain even with everybody else. Those who are afraid of others' gifting are usually insecure, competitive and jealous and want ownership of the anointing of God."[4]

We all need people to believe in us and come alongside us to boost our confidence, pulling us along. On the other hand, we need to be encouragers to come alongside others and not be dream killers ourselves. Jealousy and naysaying can be the biggest killer to another's dream. But let me reassure you that whatever God sets in motion, no man can kill. His purposes will go on regardless of what others try to do or say, as long as we humbly stay under His covering and continue on the path that He has set for us. The only one who can kill your dream is you. If you choose not to follow God's will for your life, then the dream will not happen. We can be our own worst enemy!

And so it was that in March, we pulled up stakes and headed for the Midwest, one more time into the unknown, trusting in God for every step. I felt that I had left my ministry behind and wondered how that prophecy of returning would ever come to pass...

---

[4] Jill Austin, *Dancing With Destiny*, (Grand Rapids, Michigan: Chosen Books) p.45

CHAPTER 9

Promises Fulfilled

I traversed the shaky truss bridge that spanned the Missouri River and steered my car north toward St. Charles, Missouri, a charming historic town situated along the banks of the river. I had left home that morning in anticipation of attending a Women's Aglow gathering advertised in the newspaper. We had only moved to the Midwest a couple of months prior, and I was anxious to find some like-minded Christian friends. Besides my church, here, I figured, was a good place to start. Once again, I was far from home, family, and friends, and I still smarted from having to leave my ministry behind. None of it made sense to me, but I was determined to at least search out some fellowship.

Upon locating the address, I parked my car behind the time-worn building and tentatively entered the meeting room that resounded with the happy chatter of sharply dressed women who were milling around a table laden with coffee pots and sweet rolls. I quickly assessed my surroundings. There was nothing exceptional about the somewhat outdated room other than the fact that I had noted the tile floor was unusually highly polished and glossy. Lined up in rows were lightweight metal folding chairs that faced the front podium, all readied for the meeting to get underway.

I too made my way to the refreshment table where I struck up some small talk with two ladies standing nearby. They invited me to sit with them during the service, and we chose three seats along the center aisle.

The speaker had a good message, and at the end, she invited those who wanted prayer to come forward. I bowed my head to join in prayer for those with needs when I felt a tap on my arm from the new friend who sat next to me. She said, "Um, I want to get baptized in the Holy Spirit, and I feel the Lord has said that you are to pray with me."

I was a bit startled. I had prayed over many to receive the baptism in the Holy Spirit with the evidence of speaking in tongues, but I had never mentioned anything to anyone there about my ministry background. Not only that, but this also threw me into a quandary, because I didn't deem it appropriate to take the ministry focus off the speaker, and I knew that that was frowned upon by the Aglow leadership to do so. I surely didn't want to get off on the wrong foot. I was there to make friends, not alienate myself!

In response, I smiled and whispered, "You know, I think you should go up and have the speaker pray with you." I left it at that and bowed my head in continued prayer.

A couple of minutes passed before I felt a tap on my arm again. The same lady said, "I'm sorry, but I know that you are to pray with me." She was most insistent. I shot up a quick plea to God for some wisdom and then decided that I would very quietly say a prayer over her and just try to run under the radar, so to speak, and not draw any attention to myself. That would be a little tricky, however, since those who sat directly in front of us had all gone up for prayer, and we could easily be seen from the front. But the woman was adamant. Finally, to appease her, I laid my hands on her and softly petitioned the Lord on her behalf.

Immediately, the glory of God came upon her. She shook under the Holy Spirit's power, which caused her to slip off her chair onto the floor and crash into the empty seats in front of us. That set off a domino effect with those flimsy chairs. Row after row slid across the slick, glossy tile and toppled over, triggering a major ruckus. It was like a scene right out of an "I Love Lucy Show." So much for running under the radar and not drawing attention to myself!

Every head in the room turned to see what had happened, and every eye was on us, including the group president's. She turned around and locked eyes with mine. All I could think was, *Now I've done it! I'll be jettisoned out of here and never be able to come back again.*

I tried to act nonchalant, as if nothing had happened, when suddenly, the dear lady on the floor began to loudly speak in tongues under the anointing of the Holy Spirit. Her friend got down on her knees to pray with her and others gathered around. There was nothing else for me to do to but join in.

Eventually, she was able to get up off the floor, joyfully voicing praise to the Lord, radiant with His presence. The meeting ended, and all I wanted to do was bolt out of there; but I wasn't fast enough—the president was headed my way with her entourage of board members. Beet-red with embarrassment and dreading a severe reprimand, I thought, *Here it comes...*

She righted an overturned chair and sat down across from me. "Hi," she said. "My name is Jean*." She then cocked her head to one side, squinted her eyes, and asked, "Who are you?"

I gave her a weak, mealy smile and struggled to croak out, "Hi. My name is Linda, and I just recently moved here from California."

She peered at me for a moment with her steady, cool blue eyes and said, "Noooo...who *are* you?"

I knew at that point that I was outed and needed to come clean. I nervously cleared my throat. "Well, my name is Linda Triska. My husband and I recently moved here from California," I repeated, "and I had a ministry there and..."

"I knew it! I knew it!" she triumphantly announced and looked around at her board members, who vigorously nodded their heads in agreement. She probed for more information about my ministry, and I answered as well as I could, though confused and bewildered by all of the questions.

Then she triumphantly repeated, "I knew it! The Holy Spirit told me you were in ministry and that you are to be our next speaker!" She asked me to send her a biography and sample recording of one of my messages. We exchanged numbers and other information, and I was back in ministry!

---

* Name changed.

I left the hall and sat in my car for a few moments to gain my composure before venturing out on to the road home. I cried at God's absolute goodness; I praised Him for His continued call on my life; I repented that I doubted Him; and I laughed all the way home at that deliciously absurd, divine setup of His! When God calls us, He will make a way—somehow, someway—even if He has to make a major clatter to do so.

From that booking came another open door to speak in another ministry group. And so it went. The opportunities presented themselves, and I didn't have to stress or chase after them. God's hand brought them to me.

An Addition to the Family

That summer arrived with an oppressive heat, along with an old friend from my prior Savannah days—humidity. It was difficult to get my body to readjust to it. I was nauseated every day, all day, and blamed it on the excessive heat. After a while, however, when it wouldn't relent, I became suspicious, and yes, my hunch was right. We were expecting our first child!

Our daughter, Tawny, was born one day before her due date, perfect in every way. After her birth, the invitations to speak resumed.

With Brad's travel schedule, I needed help. My dad was ready to retire from full-time ministry, so my parents pulled up stakes and moved near us. They were a Godsend, always readily available to babysit and offer assistance where needed.

The Fulfillment

A year had passed, and we celebrated Tawny's first birthday. She fell asleep during her party, and I held her in my arms as I sat on the steps and watched the other children play in our newly remodeled basement recreation room. Yep, life was good, and I was content.

I pondered over the preceding two years and marveled at how far I had come since that nerve-wracking day at the Aglow meeting in St. Charles. So much good had transpired, and my heart was filled with thanksgiving. Everything I had wanted in life was right there. I was happy and settled and had a full schedule of things I loved to do.

As far as I was concerned, I had an idyllic life. There was just nothing else I needed and nowhere else I wanted to be. I had long since let go of my dream to go back to Los Angeles; however, God had not.

Spring had come back around. The trees in our wooded backyard were in full bloom, awake from their long winter's slumber. Our little victory garden showed signs of life, with shoots peaking up from the rich Midwest soil, and on occasion, I'd catch sight of a doe crossing our three-acre property with her young ones following behind.

On the afternoon of May 22, I put Tawny down for her nap and I too went to lie down before I started dinner. I had just drifted off into a dreamless sleep when the phone next to the bed rang. Drowsily, I answered and heard Brad's familiar voice.

"Hi. What are you doing?" he asked.

"Trying to take a nap..." I lazily answered.

"Well, I have some news."

I yawned. "Okay. What?" I wasn't very interested in his news. I was more interested in getting back to my nap.

"I've been offered another promotion."

At that, my eyes flew wide open, and my heart began to pound. I cautiously asked, "Where?"

"You won't believe it, but...we're going back to Southern California!" He nervously giggled.

Now I was fully awake and sat straight up.

"I've been offered the Metropolitan Director of Division Sales position in Los Angeles, the second largest division in the country! I'll tell you more about it when I get home." We hung up with not much more said.

I grabbed my Bible lying on the nightstand next to me and feverishly thumbed to Psalm 126:5–6, the scripture I had marked two years before. "Yes, they go out weeping...and return singing." The Lord said He would bring me back, back to California...and this was the fulfillment of yet another promise.

CHAPTER 10

Homecoming

As you read this, I'm sure you thought that I exuberantly did my happy dance and immediately went to pack to rush back to California, but I did neither. As I said, I was content in the life that I had carved out there. Now I had to start again, only there was even more to deal with. This time, I would have to work around the baby's schedule, plus I knew my parents would want to move with us. There was no reason for them to stay. That meant I'd have two houses to sell, and I needed to find either two homes to buy in California or find one that would accommodate us all. It seemed a formidable task.

Brad left for California within two weeks to start in his new position, and I was left with the details of the move. I hit my knees. "Father, You know all that needs to be done and every problem I face. There's no doubt that you want us back in California, so please help me with every facet of this move." Within minutes, I heard Him answer, "Every *i* will be dotted and every *t* will be crossed, and I will not rest until it is completed." With that, I felt the anxiety leave my body and my worries quell. I took Him at His word, and with a new resolve, I faced every challenge one at a time, and the enthusiasm of going back to Los Angeles welled up within me. I was ready to "return singing."

In record time, we sold both my parent's house and ours and found the perfect residence in Orange County, California, that would accommodate our family of three plus my parents. Mom and Dad had their own fully-equipped apartment on the top floor of the house, and we lived on the main floor, having plenty of space for both families. It was as if it had been built just for us. Indeed, every *i* was dotted and every *t* crossed, just as the Father had assured us.

Once we were moved in, I contacted my old ministry buddies and, not long afterward, got a call from one of them to be on the roster for a Christian women's conference in Pomona. That booking opened a door to speak at an African-American church. I was back on my way.

Music Ministry

Another tag from the Umbrella was about to be birthed. I sat in the recording studio office in front of the owner and drew in a deep breath. "Um, I don't know if you will understand this, Tim*," I ventured, "but God spoke to me and said that you are to give me recording time—free."

In 1982, I wrote my first gospel song. It was nothing I had really aspired to do, but somehow, tunes and lyrics would charge through my thoughts, and I'd write them down. When I would go out to speak, I would oft times sing some of those songs and sometimes would write a song specifically to go along with the message.

In 1988, I met a gentleman who played keyboard and arranged music. After taking a listen to my songs, he actually liked what he heard and offered to arrange them. His idea was to do a mini album and set up bookings for me to go out to speak and sing.

I had one problem, however—I needed funds to record. The studio I had set my sights on was used by many of the Christian artists and record companies who were headquartered in Orange County at the time before most of them moved to Nashville. This studio was one of the best.

As I prayed about it, the Lord spoke to me and said that I was to tell the studio owner, Tim, that God said he was to give me the recording time for free. Now, Tim was not a believer, and I was sure that he would think I was out of my mind! If I were him, I probably would have thought that too! But God's instructions were clear-cut.

---

* Name changed.

I called my manager-agent and told him what God had said. Though he knew the studio owner, his adamant answer was, "Well, you can tell him that. I'm not!"

"All right," I agreed. "Make an appointment with Tim, and I'll tell him myself." He was dubious but made the phone call anyway and set up the meeting.

The following week, we arrived at the Costa Mesa studio and were ushered into Tim's diminutive second-floor office. We swapped some polite banter and then got down to the brass tacks of the visit.

"So what brings you here today?" Tim smiled.

My manager cleared his throat, "Well, Tim, we need some recording time for a mini-album project."

Tim matter-of-factly said, "Okay," and began to rattle off some hourly rates and recording time availability.

My manager turned to look at me as if to say, "Go ahead. Tell him."

I fidgeted in my seat, licked my dry lips, and jumped in with both feet. "Uh, Tim, I need to tell you something." My mind reeled, fervently praying that I heard correctly from the Lord.

Tim paused and quizzically looked at me, at which point I blurted out that he was to give me free recording time because God said so.

He raised his eyebrows and just stared at me. Clearly, he was taken aback. The room was dead silent, pregnant with those words hanging out in midair. I must have been crazy to have said that, I chastised myself. My thoughts were, *This man doesn't understand spiritual things, and I've really put him on the spot.*

Suddenly, the atmosphere in the room changed. He leaned back in his chair, clasped his hands behind his head, and said with a wry smile, "Well, if God said that's what we're to do, then I guess we better do it." He proceeded to offer some available recording times, introduced us to the engineer he would assign to the project, shook our hands, and it was a done deal. Talk about shock and awe!

I walked out of the studio into the sun-drenched California afternoon in a daze. The Holy Spirit had already gone ahead and worked it all out to my good. The scripture in Jeremiah 29:11 (NIV) streaked through my mind, " 'For I know the plans I have for you,' declares the Lord, 'plans to prosper you and not to harm you, plans to give you hope and a future.' "

Once the album was complete, I sold it at my mini concerts and meetings, but I never felt called to a full-on Christian music career. It was more of an enhancement to the centerpiece of my ministry of speaking and prayer.

Tawny

As the years rushed on, our daughter was growing up, and keeping up with her activities was getting to be a challenge. The Lord blessed her with an amazing singing talent. She eventually got an entertainment agent, and the auditioning began. She and I did a lot of duets early on, and then she was off booking on her own. But her story is for her to tell.

As her career began to take off, it was apparent that I couldn't keep both my ministry and her activities going simultaneously. There were times I would have a speaking engagement, and at the same time, she would get called for an audition. Weighed down by it all, I finally got before the Lord and cried out, "Father, I can't keep all of this going this way. I love being a mom and being with my daughter. I only have one child, and I want to be involved with her while she's growing up. So I'm asking you to release me from ministry for now, and when she's raised, I promise I will come back to it." It was a hard prayer, and I didn't make that decision lightly. However, I believe that God knows a mother's heart. As a result, the doors shut, and God honored my request. Over those years, I did have opportunities to go out and minister on occasion, but it was certainly not at the pace that it had been.

By the time Tawny turned eighteen, she wanted to be on her own, and Manager-Mom was no longer needed. I had to put her in God's hands and let her fly. As a parent, I think it is one of the hardest things we ever have to do. The empty-nest syndrome was very real and painful to me, especially because of the fact that I was so enmeshed in her life—so much so that I had lost track of who I was. I struggled for a year, wondering where I was to go from there. I prayed and wept as I tried to breach the waters of my sea of despair and confusion.

New Beginnings

The Father was gracious to allow me to raise my daughter and be mom and wife in the way that I had requested. Six years earlier, Brad had left Kellogg's after twenty-three years, and we purchased a business in Laguna Beach. I worked there with him and tried some other avenues, but everything felt flat.

It was around that time that Brad and I both felt restless and sensed that the Spirit of the Lord was leading us out of Orange County. We needed to start fresh. The year before, we had put our business up for sale, but there wasn't a single offer to purchase. Now, a year later, it was God's timing, and we had five buyers in line. We quickly sold the business and then set the house up for sale. It sold within two weeks! There was one problem, though. We had received no direction as to where we were to move. The Lord was yet to reveal that to us, and time was getting short with both the business and our home ready to close escrow.

We spent our days off scouring the highways and byways of Southern California. We would drive to various areas of the Southland, asking the Lord, "Is this it?" as we went along, but nothing seemed to fit—that is, until we visited the California High Desert, situated between Los Angeles and Las Vegas, Nevada. We knew this is where the Lord was leading us, but why here? Orange County was green and lush, and the High Desert was…well…a desert—brown and dry with extreme weather. It was one of those "never" places. Whenever we would travel through that area, I'd say, "I'd never want to live here." I can tell you now that I *never* say never anymore! Yet we knew God was affirming that this is where He wanted us.

We contacted a realtor and found the perfect house and transferred our lives from the familiar of eighteen years to the desert. As we made our way up the Cajon Pass the day we moved, I wondered what God had up His sleeve this time. A whole new chapter was before us, waiting to be discovered in "never land."

A Deal's A Deal

I was still trying to figure out why I was in the desert. What exactly was I doing here?

"Okay, God," I would cry out. "What do you want?"

In August 2007, my answer came with force and clarity. It was on a Sunday night as I was driving home alone from church that I heard God speak once again.

He simply said, "She's rai-aised," in a sing-song voice. "A deal's a deal!" And I knew immediately what He meant. I was reminded that I had beseeched the Lord when my daughter was young to allow me to raise her and promised that when she became an adult, I would come back to full-time ministry. God was calling me to make good on the deal I had made with Him. He has a long memory, and now that my daughter was of age, He came collecting!

At that point, I was ready, and I told Him so but reminded Him that He would have to open the doors again. I left it at that and motored on home, wondering how on earth He would make it happen this time. But again, the Father doesn't run out of ideas.

My next challenge was that the gifts I had operated in had somewhat waned over the years. The more we work at something in the natural realm, the better we get at it. This also holds true in the spiritual realm. The more we foster our gifts by exercising them with prayer, the more we activate the anointing and become more proficient at those gifts. Conversely, should we not work at those things, they will diminish. I knew I needed a shot of *dunamis* (power) to refuel my Holy Spirit tank, and it came through a young evangelist named David Tomberlin, in a power bomb that kick-started my ministry once again.

An Appointment with the Holy Spirit

A weekend conference was being held in Pasadena, California, and evangelist David Tomberlin was on the speaking roster. On that Saturday, David had set up a luncheon and was offering prayer for those interested in ministry activation. Well, I was definitely interested in that! We were invited to come to the front, and I opted to sit on the floor. David went down the row and poured oil into each of our hands as he prayed over us. As the oil was poured over my palms, dripping down my arms and onto the floor, the Spirit of God hit me like an explosion! I fell over flat on my face, going down in slow motion, and stayed there for quite a while, enjoying God's manifest presence wrapped around me.

My friends, with whom I had attended the conference, tried to pull me up, but I was still under the *kabowd* (the Hebrew word for the manifest weighty glory of God) and was unsteady on my feet. My legs gave way, and this time, I fell flat on my back. At that point, I began to feel what I can only describe as lightning strikes going through my body. They would start at the top of my head and shoot down to my feet, causing me to shake and shudder. It was waves of glory! As soon as I had recuperated from one strike, another would start. These strikes did not harm me in any way nor was I unconscious. When under the anointing of the Spirit, people can still be aware of the world around them unless they are transported into a heavenly realm; but because the Holy Spirit's power is so strong, our human bodies will react in one way or another to that power.

I lay there in His presence for about forty-five minutes and then was finally able to crawl over to a chair and climb up to the seat, trying to collect my senses. I was intoxicated by the Holy Spirit's power. Later that night, while lying in my bed, I was visited again by the holy shockwaves until the morning light brought quietness to my body and soul.

This visitation reactivated the anointing on my life and ministry, and the gifts returned in power and authority. I wrote in my journal that I truly believed that "this weekend was the kick off." Once more, I began to experience salvations, healings, deliverances, and signs and wonders when I prayed for others, only this time in greater measure than ever before. The Holy Spirit had just been waiting for my "yes" again.

Now I was prepared and equipped "for every good work" (2 Timothy 3:17). Not long afterward, to my astonishment, the president of an Aglow chapter, where I had spoken once before, called and asked if I'd be interested in speaking at another monthly meeting. The opportunities did indeed present themselves again.

Once the Holy Spirit puts a call on our lives, He will never change His mind; it holds throughout our lifetime. That is clearly stated in Romans 11:29 (NLT): "For God's gifts and his call can never be withdrawn." Even if we are running away from the call, we will continue to feel that pull and hear that voice calling us to God's purposes and plans for our life. Frankly, the Holy Spirit is relentless!

New doors began to open for me to teach on spiritual gifts again at weekend conferences and retreats, ministry groups, and churches, which formally birthed the "Targeting Your Spiritual Gifts" series. It was developed over time, step by step, through a process and came to fruition—another fulfillment of a spoke tag on the Umbrella.

Feed My Sheep

Now I was ready to officially establish my ministry and ride off into the sunset with Jesus. However, He had another job that He needed me to take care of before I was to move fully in that direction.

Immediately before we left Orange County, while seeking God's plan for us in the desert, I had a dream. I saw a church that had a gymnasium. Situated at the far end of the gym was a purple carpeted portable stage. On the stage were people distributing food to those in need. Those on the stage beckoned to me when they saw me enter the door, saying, "Come and help us," similar to the Apostle Paul's call to Macedonia in Acts 16. As I was coming out of the dream, I heard a voice state, "And this ministry is called Feed My Sheep."

I shared the dream with my husband the next morning telling him that I thought we would be helping in a food ministry at a church when we transferred to the desert. Little did I know...

The truck purchased for the food pantry, "Feed My Sheep"

Once we settled in, we began our search for a home church. We visited Victorville First Assembly of God one Sunday morning. Hmmm—it kind of looked like the church I saw in my dream. We felt compelled to visit a second time, and on that Sunday, we were invited to return for the evening service and attend a visitor's welcome gathering afterward. It was being held in the gym of their Christian school, which was located on the same campus. We did not know at the time that there was a school, let alone a gymnasium!

Now we were curious. We had to find out. We agreed to attend, and when we walked into that gym, there it was, at the far end of the room—a portable purple carpeted stage exactly as I saw it in my dream!

I asked around to ascertain whether there was a food pantry ministry at the church but was startled to find out that there was none. How could that be? This was definitely the church I had seen in the dream. I just couldn't understand it until one day, while working around my house, I heard the Spirit of the Lord say that I was to establish Feed My Sheep Ministries.

"Oh no, Lord! Not me! I like what I'm doing—going out speaking. Anyway, I have no experience with managing a food outreach, not to mention I can see this will be a lot of work, and I wouldn't be able to book many speaking engagements if I do this. Please call someone else who needs something to do." But argue as I might, I kept hearing, "Establish Feed My Sheep."

One evening, I very tentatively mentioned it to Brad. To my dismay, he immediately said, "Well then, we better go talk to the pastor." That's not what I wanted to hear at all, but I made the appointment and went into the meeting, hoping the pastor would say there's no storage room at the church for a food pantry or something, anything, to get me out of it. But the pastor was all for it. God had deemed it, and therefore, it was to be.

I was really puzzled by this new call, though. I thought He had called me, anointed me, and equipped me to go out to speak and pray for the sick. So why was I on this detour? The Spirit of God did answer that question. He had called others to set up a food ministry in that church, but no one would heed the call. As a matter of fact, I had a couple of people admit to me later that they knew they were called to start it, but didn't heed the call. There were many in the High Desert region that needed help, and the Lord was poised to answer their cries. He just needed someone's "yes."

We all have a main call on our lives as mentioned earlier, but sometimes, there will also be a secondary call when the Lord needs someone to accomplish a temporary task or fill a spot that another has refused to fulfill. Feed My Sheep in the High Desert (now the official non-profit name) was a secondary call for me.

Sharon Marson, a lady who was familiar with the non-profit sector and was a grant writer, joined ranks with me. She was exactly the person I needed to help navigate that whole new world. Within five years, Feed My Sheep in the High Desert became one of the largest food pantries in the region, feeding thousands of people each year. I'm pleased to say that it is still going strong and continues to feed those in distress throughout the region.

I didn't know what I was doing when I started the pantry, but the Lord was in it. He loves to stretch us beyond what we think we can do. There have been times that I've felt like that rubber toy, Gumby, being pulled, stretched, and bent in different shapes. But by that pulling, stretching, and bending, the Father shapes us into the vessel that He wants us to be for His glory and purposes.

In the midst of the mounds of work in the food pantry, the Lord still continued to open doors for me to go out and speak. Somehow, I was able to keep up with it all, and after five years, the Lord released me from Feed My Sheep with the instructions to officially establish my own ministry, It's Beginning to Rain, where I had my own food distribution ministry.

Another Umbrella Spoke Fulfilled

I stared at the email I had just opened. I read and reread it a couple of times to make sure I understood it correctly. It was from a friend in Orange County who stated that a gentleman from her church had launched a new television broadcasting network and was looking for programming. She went on to say that she had immediately thought of me and wanted to know if I'd be interested in developing a new show.

On the set of the television show, "It's Beginning to Rain"

My mind whirled back to January of that same year (2016). The Lord had spoken to me and said I would birth something new in March. It was March when I opened the email. My mind spun further back to October 29, 1984, when I'd had the vision of the Umbrella. I ran to pull out the drawing I had sketched of it. Yes, there it was! One of the spoke tags read, "TV Show." However, what was even more telling was a vision that I had Sunday morning, October 28, 2007, confirming that this show would come to pass. Very specifically, God revealed to me a television talk show that I would host, interviewing various guests which I was to call "It's Beginning to Rain," now the name of my ministry as well.

I contacted the broadcaster, and after meeting with him, I knew this was the appointed time that was on heaven's calendar. Thirty-two years after the initial prophecy, the show was born. Many times throughout the intervening years, I wondered why I had taken all of those film classes. Even after receiving those television prophecies, I just couldn't see it. But God was working out His blueprint for my life.

Friends, God is not a man that He would lie, and that which has been promised will come to pass in due season. It won't necessarily be on our timetable, but when He deems it so, it will happen. There were times when I wondered if any of the promises prophesied to me would happen. But they have! And they will for you as well. God says in Psalms that He magnifies His Word even above His name. Not one word that He has spoken will fall to the ground unanswered. You will see a fulfillment of those promises if you stay in fellowship with Him and seek His will for your life.

There have been six tags on the Umbrella that have indeed come to pass, with two still to be fulfilled. I know that the two remaining will happen in God's time and God's way. Do I know how? No, I don't because they too seem so big and out of my realm, but I know they will become a reality because I have seen His hand at work throughout my life, starting with a little girl from Nowhere, USA, who dreamed big ridiculous dreams. When God breathes in our direction, it doesn't matter where we come from, what kind of degrees we have or don't have, or whether we have any kind of personal connections. He will equip us with every gifting necessary to accomplish the call and destiny mapped out for us and will ready us for the last days revival that I believe is just on the other side of tomorrow. All we need is the courage to step out and an obedient heart that follows after the Father.

The last days revival will not be led by big name ministries as revivals have been in the past but by the "ordinaries" who are willing to lay it all on the line for the Gospel of the Kingdom of God. They will be considered unlikely candidates, according to this world's standards. And the Holy Spirit is preparing His Church right now to be ready when that door flies open. Now is the time to learn and train as warriors on the front lines. The harvest will be abundant, and many laborers will be needed to reap the souls in the field of God.

You are called to join His army. I don't believe for a second that you have read this book by accident or coincidence but, rather, by the leading of God's hand. Therefore, gear up! Get ready! Dream God's dreams and chase after the One who knows your tomorrows.

***

I have shared my journey here with you in the hopes of inspiring you to pursue your own journey with Jesus. He is no respecter of persons. What He has done in my life, He will do in yours, as well.

In this next section, we will explore how you too can find your gifts and, ultimately, your purpose and destiny. The Lord is just waiting for you to say, "Yes, Lord! Send me."

THE FAMILY ROOM

My grandparents, John, Constance, Philomena, and Michael

My son-in-law and daughter, Hunter and Tawny

My brothers, Ken, Rick and me

My parents, Sam and Mary

Brad and me

SECTION 2

Targeting Your Spiritual Gifts

The Lord will fulfill his purposes for me; your love, O Lord, endures forever—do not abandon the works of your hands.

—Psalm 138:8 (NIV)

CHAPTER 11

Who Is the Holy Spirit?

Profile of the Holy Spirit

Before we explore the gifts of the Spirit, it's important that we identify and understand who the Holy Spirit is and understand His purpose on earth. The scriptures mention many job descriptions of the Spirit of God, but for the purpose of this book, I want to highlight what Jesus says about Him in John 14. "And I will ask the Father, and He will give you another Comforter (Counselor, Helper, Intercessor, Advocate, Strengthener, and Standby) that He may remain with you forever...The Spirit of Truth, Whom the world cannot receive (welcome, take to its heart), because it does not see Him or know and recognize Him. But you know and recognize Him, for He lives with you [constantly] and will be in you" (John 14:16–17, AMPC).

The word "Comforter" used in this passage in the original Greek is the word *Paracletos*, meaning "one called to the side of another for the purpose of helping in any way." Jesus told us that He would not leave us "high and dry" but would send the Holy Spirit, the Helper, to come alongside us. Nothing is too great for the Holy Spirit to handle and nothing is too small to call for His help. People laugh when I tell them I pray for parking spots. Living in jam-packed Southern California makes it difficult to find parking almost everywhere I go. But guess what? I always find a parking spot! If something concerns us, it concerns Him. He is "with" us, constantly factoring into our lives and accompanying us wherever we go. What a comforting thought!

That verse also goes on to say that He will not only be "with" us but will also be "in" us, signaling that there would be a Holy Spirit infilling. He will take up residence in us as believers. In this scripture, Jesus was pointing to the Acts 2 experience of the Spirit's power dwelling in us to first of all, make us more into Christ's image to produce the fruit of the Spirit in our lives listed in Galatians 5:22—love, joy, peace, longsuffering, gentleness, goodness, faith, meekness, and temperance.

The *fruit of the Spirit* should not be confused with the *gifts of the Spirit*. The fruit of the Spirit is the measuring stick of our *maturity* in Christ. The way we live our lives demonstrates our Christlikeness (or not) through our thoughts, words, and deeds. Jesus said in Matthew 7:20 (NLT), "Yes, the way to identify a tree or a person is by the kind of fruit that is produced."

Also note that it is the *fruit* of the Spirit, singular, not plural, indicating that all of those named in Galatians 5:22 are to be dealt with as a whole. It's not à la carte, where we pick and choose which ones work for us and which don't! The Lord wants all of the fruit to be evident in our lives. They are to be viewed as a whole, like an orange—one piece of fruit but made up of several segments.

A self-examination of how well we are reflecting the fruit of the Spirit in our personal lives is available in the separate workbook that complements this text. The questions will help identify what we have conquered and what needs work.

Also, when the Spirit dwells in us, He will produce *power*, power to serve by equipping us with the gifts needed to fulfill the unique call that is on each Christian's life, and the power to perform the same signs, wonders, and miracles that Jesus did to back up His Word while on earth. Through these works, we become His witnesses. So as the fruit of the Spirit is about spiritual growth and maturity, the gifts of the Spirit are about power and service.

The Spirit's power was evident at the creation. We see in Genesis 1:2 that it was the Spirit of God who hovered over the water to bring form to the earth. God spoke the word to create, and the Spirit, by

His mighty power, created that which was spoken. The Spirit of God is the power of God with no beginning and no end, as God Himself. He is, therefore, a member of the Holy Trinity comprised of God the Father, God the Son and God the Holy Spirit, yet it must be understood that it is God manifesting as three equal persons. Each member represents a different facet of Jehovah: God the Father represents God's rule, God the Son represents God's love and God the Spirit represents God's power.

Also, in Genesis 1:26 (NAS), God said, "Let Us make man in Our image, according to Our likeness." To whom was He speaking? Not the angels—they are created beings. He had to have spoken to those of equal preeminence and eternal existence. As already stated, the Spirit and the Father are mentioned in the beginning in Genesis 1:2, but what of Jesus, the Son? The first part of John 1:1–3 (NIV) makes the deity of Christ clear: "In the beginning was the Word, and the Word was with God, and the Word was God. He was with God in the beginning. Through him all things were made; without him nothing was made that has been made." Jesus is the Word and the fulfillment of the Word!

Additionally, we see all three members of the Godhead manifest at the water baptism of Jesus, relayed in Matthew 3. Jesus was in the flesh, God's voice was heard from Heaven, and the Holy Spirit appeared as a dove. This was the only account ever recorded in the Word where the three separate entities were made known at one time. It was also a holy moment of God's confirmation and infusing of power upon Jesus, which launched Him into His three-and-a-half-year miracle-working ministry on earth. At that point, though Jesus was fully God, yet He was also fully man and needed that empowerment while on the earth. Clothed with power from on high, Jesus was ready then to begin His public ministry. If Jesus needed the Holy Spirit's power, then how much more do we?!

Characteristics of the Holy Spirit

Often the Spirit is referred to as *It*; however, Jesus referred to the Holy Spirit as *He*, as seen in John 16:13 (NAS): "But when He, the

Spirit of truth, comes, He will guide you into all the truth;" We can then say that He is a Being and, therefore, has characteristics. The Word states that He has a mind (Romans 8:27), He has knowledge (1 Corinthians 2:11), He has a will (1 Corinthians 12:11), and He has emotions (Romans 15:30), i.e., He can be grieved (Ephesians 4:30) and He is jealous over us (James 4:5). However, He has no revealed personal name. Why? The answer lies in the continuance of John 16: "...for He will not speak on His own initiative, but whatever He hears, He will speak; and He will disclose to you what is to come. He will glorify Me, for He will take of Mine and will disclose it to you. All things that the Father has are Mine; therefore, I said that He takes of Mine and will disclose it to you" John 16:13b–15 (NAS).

Thus, His name is withheld so that the name of Jesus is exalted. That is why we pray in the name of Jesus. We pray His name and the Spirit of God moves within that name to bring glory to the Son and the Son gives glory to the Father.

Now that we've discussed the deity of the Holy Spirit and His power, how does He personally relate to us, and how do we activate His power in our own lives? That question is addressed in the next chapter.

CHAPTER 12

Why Do I Need the Baptism in the Holy Spirit?

> But you will receive power when the Holy Spirit comes
> on you; and you will be my witnesses in Jerusalem, and in
> all Judea and Samaria, and to the ends of the earth.

—Acts 1:8 (NIV)

The above scripture records the last words of Jesus to His disciples before He ascended back to the Father in heaven, so they must have been pretty important. He had also mentioned the "promise of the Father" (Acts 1:4–5) just a few days prior to this, and throughout the Gospels, there were many references to the arrival of the Holy Spirit. The Lord wanted to make that message clear because of the great significance and necessity of the Spirit's power to carry on the work He had begun on earth. The disciples would need power and would receive it through the Holy Spirit.

Jesus told his disciples to go directly to Jerusalem and to wait there until they received this baptism. "For John baptized with water, but in a few days you will be baptized with the Holy Spirit" Acts 1:5 (NIV). I'm sure the disciples didn't know what to expect, but out of obedience, anticipation, and probably a little curiosity, they followed their Master's instructions.

The backdrop to the story is that Jesus did not ascend to the Father immediately after His resurrection but remained on earth for forty days to reveal Himself as the resurrected Messiah to His disciples and to over 500 believers (1 Corinthians 15:6). During that time period, He commissioned His disciples to wait in Jerusalem for this gift. It was vital that they be endued with power through the Holy Spirit before they went out to minister, just as Jesus had been empowered.

The disciples immediately left for Jerusalem and waited there for ten days after Jesus's ascension, which put them at the time of the Feast of Pentecost, a Jewish festival celebrated fifty days after Passover. (Pentecost in the Greek means "fiftieth.") All Jewish men were required to attend three feasts in Jerusalem each year—Passover (Pesach), Pentecost (Shavuot), and Tabernacles (Sukkot). These feasts were actually symbolic of coming events set on God's timetable, or what is known as "types and shadows" of things to come, each to be fulfilled at God's appointed time. The death and resurrection of Jesus during Passover was the fulfillment of that feast as the final and ultimate sacrifice—the Lamb of God. Jesus said He came to fulfill the Law (Matthew 5:17). Pentecost was about to be fulfilled as well.

Pentecost, also known as Shavuot, Feast of Weeks, and Feast of Harvest, was a celebration of the grain harvests (see Deuteronomy 16:9–10) and a foreshadowing of the coming harvest of souls. When the Holy Spirit came into the upper room and baptized the 120 followers of Christ with His power, it birthed the New Testament Church to become witnesses to bring in the harvest of souls. When we are baptized in the Holy Spirit, He imparts power to us to be witnesses through our testimony and service in His Kingdom. That power, the exact same power that raised Christ from the dead, is deposited in us by the Holy Spirit to accomplish all that He has assigned us to do as His witnesses.

Three Types of Baptisms

There are three distinct baptisms noted in the scriptures. The word baptism simply means "to submerge or immerse." In 1 Corinthians 12:13 (NIV), we find the first baptism: "For we were all baptized by one Spirit into one body—whether Jews or Greeks, slave or free—and we were all given the one Spirit to drink." When we receive Christ into our hearts as our Savior and Lord, we are baptized, or submerged, *by* the Spirit into one body—the Body of Christ.

The second baptism is baptism *in* water, first indicated in Matthew 3:16 (NIV) when John the Baptist came on the scene and baptized Jesus in the Jordan River: "As soon as Jesus was baptized, he went up out of the water." We too, as believers, should be baptized, fully immersed in water, as Jesus was, for He is our example. This is an indicator to the world that our sins are forgiven and buried, and we are followers of the Messiah.

The third baptism is the Act 2 experience: baptism *with* or *in* the Holy Spirit. This is an immersion in the Holy Spirit. When we are saved through the blood of Jesus Christ, scripture states that we are sealed by the Spirit (Ephesians 1:13-14). We receive a portion of the Spirit at that time, but it does not indicate submergence. The baptism in the Holy Spirit is a subsequent blessing after we become believers. "...Paul having passed through the upper coasts came to Ephesus: and finding certain *disciples*, he said unto them, Have ye received the Holy Ghost *since* ye believed?" (Acts 19:1-2, KJV; emphasis added). Therefore, we see here that this experience is after, and in addition to, salvation.

The Day of Pentecost

As 120 followers of Jesus were congregated in the upstairs room of a home in Jerusalem on the day of Pentecost, the Word of God says that the Holy Spirit entered with the sound of a rushing mighty wind and with flames of fire that rested upon each person's head. The Holy Spirit made an entrance that even Hollywood couldn't have rivaled! There was no doubt that He had arrived. But it didn't stop there. Acts 2:4 (NLT) goes on to say that all there were "filled with the Holy Spirit and began speaking in other languages, as the Holy Spirit gave them this ability." They were praising God in languages they had never learned as the Holy Spirit gave them the ability to do so. And what a commotion they made! So much so that it attracted a crowd outside the house, which gave Peter the opportunity to preach his first sermon. The Spirit changed him from being fearful and intimidated (remember, he denied Jesus three times) to being full of boldness and power, and 3,000 souls were added to the Kingdom of God that day!

The word power used here in the Greek is "*dunamis.*" In Abingdon's *Strong's Exhaustive Concordance of the Bible, dunamis* is described as "miraculous power." The English word "dynamite" is rooted in this same word. This power is inherent in the person of the Holy Spirit. It's who He is—all power!

Is Speaking in Tongues for Today?

There is a great deal of controversy concerning the baptism of the Holy Spirit with the physical evidence of speaking in tongues. The fact that the 120 believers all spoke in languages they had never learned (known in the Greek as glossolalia) was a sign that they were indeed baptized in the Holy Spirit. There was no guesswork or indecisiveness as to whether they received it. It was the evidence that they had received the Holy Spirit infilling. This was repeated in Acts 10:44–47 and Acts 19:1–7. However, the question is often posed nowadays if this gift is still for today or did it cease after the first century church age?

The doctrine which holds that the baptism of the Holy Spirit and spiritual gifts ceased at the end of the first century is known as cessationism. However, when Peter preached on the day of Pentecost, he made the statement that the promise of the Holy Spirit is for "you and your children and for all who are afar off—for all whom the Lord our God will call" (Acts 2:39, NIV). Note that the context is speaking of generations to come. It is for all who are called by God, all who are His followers. I don't believe that the Lord thought the first century church needed the power of the Holy Spirit more than we do in this age, especially as we get closer to His return. The days will become darker and more difficult, and we will need the empowerment of the Holy Spirit to strengthen us to stand in the midst of the increasing sin and turmoil. We are, therefore, specifically told,

"…do not forbid speaking in tongues." (1 Corinthians 14:39, NIV), and so, speaking in tongues continues today.

Is Speaking in Tongues From God?

It has also been disputed that tongues is not of God but of the devil. I'm confused by this statement, as Jesus himself affirmed in Mark 16:17 (KJV): "And these signs shall follow them that believe: In my name…they shall speak with new tongues." It's a supernatural sign and available to all those who have received salvation. That's pretty plain.

Personally, I believe Satan seeds that lie in order to instill fear and thereby cause rejection of the practice of speaking in tongues. He knows if the worldwide Church really got a hold of this power, his kingdom would indeed be in great trouble! The good news, however, is that Pentecostals and Charismatics are the fastest-growing religious movement in the world, and tongue-talking is being more accepted and readily embraced.

Is Speaking in Tongues Made-Up Words?

When those in the upper room spoke in tongues, it was as the Spirit gave them utterance. I heard a comment once that speaking in tongues is just a bunch of man-made gibberish. It might sound that way to those who have not had the experience, but amazingly, science has actually proven it otherwise.

In 2006, the University of Pennsylvania took brain images of five people while they were speaking in tongues. Dr. Andrew Newberg, who headed up the study, published his research conclusions in *The New York Times*. It was found that when these subjects were praying in tongues, "their frontal lobes, the willful part of the brain we use to think and control what we do, were quiet. The language center of their brains—the part we used to speak in our native language—were quiet as well."[5] Clearly, this confirms that tongues

---

[5]   http://www.nytimes.com/2006/11/07/health/07brain.html?

is a download of the Holy Spirit into our spirit, which enables us to speak in a heavenly language and bypasses our natural brain activity. We are speaking directly to God. "For anyone who speaks in tongues does not speak to men but to God." (1 Corinthians 14:2, NIV). It is a direct line into heaven's throne room.

Speaking in tongues is for our personal benefit (edification) for worship, praise, and prayer when we don't know how to pray. "And the Holy Spirit helps us in our distress. For we don't even know what we should pray for, nor how we should pray. But the Holy Spirit prays for us with groanings that cannot be expressed in words. And the Father who knows all hearts knows what the Spirit is saying, for the Spirit pleads for us believers in harmony with God's will." (Romans 8:26–27, NLT). The Spirit of God will pray the perfect prayer in line with God's will through us (through our tongues) when we don't know what to pray or how to pray.

Please note that this is not the same as the *gift of tongues*, which is a public gift for the benefit of the Church and must be interpreted in order that all can understand what is being said. Praying in tongues in our personal prayer time does not require interpretation, though there may be times when the Spirit of God will make our prayer known to us. However, obviously, one cannot operate in the gift of tongues without the ability to speak in tongues, but the gift of tongues is an increased anointing, the next level up, if you will, in the gift. The gift of tongues will be further discussed in Chapter 18 on the "Nine Supernatural Gifts of the Spirit."

Is Speaking in Tongues for Me?

If you are a follower of Christ, then the baptism in the Holy Spirit evidenced with speaking in tongues is for you! I have prayed for many who have received their prayer language and have seen their lives change dramatically by His power.

One incident stands out of a lady I prayed for on a Sunday night. She was an alcoholic and wanted to be freed of that addiction that held her captive. At the end of the message, I spotted her in the very last pew wearing large sunglasses. I knew she was in trouble. I motioned for her to come forward, and she slowly made her way down the aisle, holding on to each pew to steady herself. She collapsed on the front seat and began to sob, throwing herself across my lap with the desperate cry, "I want to be free!" The smell of alcohol overwhelmed and nauseated me. I steered her up to the altar and talked to her about the gift of salvation. She said she was ready to make Jesus her Lord and Savior and prayed the sinners' prayer with me. I pressed on and told her that she also needed the power of the Holy Spirit to break all the chains of bondage off her.

As she worshipped the Lord with hands raised, she began to speak out, haltingly at first, and then the words of heaven flowed out from her innermost being. As we rejoiced with her, she gave me a hug, and incredibly, there was no alcohol odor on her breath at all and she was completely sober! She was instantaneously liberated by being filled with the Holy Spirit! I heard later that she was attending a local church and continued to walk in freedom.

The baptism in the Holy Spirit isn't just a "one-hit wonder" or a checkmark on our bucket list. We should use our prayer language every day. It will edify us personally and makes us spiritually strong. It empowers us to be bold witnesses and equips us with spiritual gifts to fulfill our destiny.

You might ask if you need this experience to make it into heaven. No, the scriptures do not teach that; however, I would hope that we all would want everything that God has for us!

How Do I Receive the Baptism in the Holy Spirit?

1. First and foremost, to receive the baptism of the Holy Spirit we must repent of our sins. Peter says in his Day of Pentecost sermon to the Jews, "Repent and be baptized, every one of you, in the name of Jesus Christ for the forgiveness of your sins. And you will receive the gift of the Holy Spirit." (Acts 2:38, NIV). Repentance for our sins and asking Christ into our hearts is what brings salvation. The Spirit cannot dwell in an unrepentant heart.

If you don't know Jesus as your Lord and Savior, tell Him you are sorry for your sins and ask His forgiveness. Then invite Him into your heart to be the Savior and Lord of your life. He says in Revelation 3 that He stands at our heart's door and knocks, but we are the ones who have to open the door and ask Him in. The latch is on the inside. We have been given freewill, and He will not cross that. He waits for the invitation. Once we've made that commitment to Him, He will wash our souls clean, change our desires, and give us eternal life with Him in heaven when we pass from this life to the next.

2. Once you have repented of your sins, ask Him to baptize you in His precious Holy Spirit. He wants us to have this gift more than we even desire it. We must believe His promise that He will fill the hungry heart. "If you, then, though you are evil, know how to give good gifts to your children, how much more will your Father in heaven give good gifts to those who ask him!" (Matthew 7:11, NIV). As a parent, I loved Christmas morning when my daughter was a child and would first see the gifts under the tree. The pure delight on her face gave me the same delight. How much more our Heavenly Father, the ultimate parent, takes pure delight in giving His children the gift of the infilling of the Holy Spirit that He has promised.

3. When desiring the Spirit's baptism, raise your hands and worship and praise God aloud. As you do this, it creates an atmosphere for the Holy Spirit's presence to manifest. It doesn't matter where you are. I've heard stories of people who were worshipping and praising God in their cars and received their prayer language going down the highway! As I had mentioned in Chapter 1, my dad was baptized in the Holy Spirit and began speaking in tongues while kneeling at the toilet!

   If you are seeking this gift, begin to worship Him right now, and He will meet you where you are. Then cooperate with Him by speaking out the words that come to you.

They may sound strange at first, but remember, these are heavenly words, and they won't necessarily sound like any words you have ever heard nor will they sound like anyone else's. They will be unique to you!

4. We receive this gift by faith. The Spirit of God will fill us up with His presence to enable us to speak in a language we've never learned and give us His power, but it takes faith on our part to open our mouths and speak it out. It is our choice to speak or not. Faith has two parts—God's part and ours. When we speak in our prayer language, it sounds strange because it's…well…out of this world; however, we must cooperate with Him if we want all that He has for us.

The Spirit is an infinite well from which God wants us to drink deeply. There is so much more available in God once we receive this power. It will open up another avenue that offers spiritual gifts for the equipping of the saints. These gifts are vehicles that will transport us into the destiny that God planned for us. Let's take a look.

CHAPTER 13

He Comes Bearing (Spiritual) Gifts

"But what are my spiritual gifts and what does God want me to do?" wailed the young woman who sat across from me, dabbing the tears that welled up in her eyes. She looked at me in despair, hoping I would have the answer.

Throughout the years of my ministry, this is arguably the most frequent question I am asked by other Christians. People are searching for their purpose and want to know how in the world they can discover their destiny. I well understand their dilemma because it was certainly one I once wrestled with as well.

We Are All Called

Because God is our Creator, then it stands to reason that we go to His Word to begin our quest to find why we are here. Ephesians 2:10 (NLT; emphasis added) conveys it quite clearly: "For we are Gods masterpiece. He has created us anew in Christ Jesus, *so that we can do the good things he planned for us long ago.*"

When we are saved, we are made into a new creation in Christ Jesus and are each called by God to do "good works" that He prepared for us to do long before we were born. God spoke in Jeremiah 1:4 (NLT), " 'I knew you before I formed you in your mother's womb. Before you were born I set you apart and appointed you…' " Each of us was created from a unique, one-of-a-kind blueprint designed by God to serve in the Body of Christ in a particular way. That is our destiny.

Therefore, we who are in the Body of Christ, the Church (*Ekklesia* in the Greek), are all called to serve God in some capacity by serving others. Jesus came to serve, not to be served. He only did what He saw the Father do. He is our example; therefore, we are to live out our lives in the same manner. He went about doing good, preaching, healing, setting the captives free, lifting up the oppressed and brokenhearted, giving, feeding, and humbly serving others to point them to the Kingdom of Heaven. That is our mandate as well—to continue that which He established in His earthly ministry.

When Jesus ascended to heaven, He sent His Holy Spirit down to earth to help us carry on His work as witnesses of the Gospel by empowering us for ministry. The Greek word for ministry is *diakonos*, which simply means "to serve." Hence, every believer is called to some type of ministry.

Holy Spirit Empowered

As previously noted, the Holy Spirit is the power arm of the Holy Trinity, and when we receive the Holy Spirit's power, it enables us to do that which we have been preordained to do. Remember, Jesus told His disciples to go straight to Jerusalem after His ascension and not leave until they were endued by the *dunamis* of the Holy Spirit before they went out to minister. Following the Pentecostal experience, we see further into the Book of Acts that the apostles then went out with the anointing of the Spirit, mightily preaching, bringing thousands to salvation, and performing the same signs and wonders as their Master. We, too, are to be clothed in power from on high to become carriers of His presence.

Functioning in the Body of Christ

The Body of Christ is a superorganism. Dictionary.com defines superorganism as "any complex thing or system having properties and functions determined not only by the properties and relations of its individual parts, but by the character of the whole that they compose and by the relations of the parts to the whole." In other words,

Christ's Body is made up of many parts, each having a specific duty which contributes to the whole.

In order to accomplish all that He has predestined us to do, the Spirit of God comes with spiritual gifts or abilities (charismata) that He equips us with to correspond with the call. Peter states in 1 Peter 4:10 (NAS) that each of us has a spiritual gift: "As each one has received a special gift, employ it in serving one another as good stewards of the manifold grace of God." We see in this scripture then, that every believer is downloaded with at least one gift. I must say, however, that the Spirit of God is lavish and distributes several gifts to each one. We will all have gift-mixes that will enable us to accomplish much in the Body of Christ.

Spiritual Gifts 101

Spiritual gifts are only for the believer and are imparted only after our spiritual birth when we become members in the Body of Christ. These gifts bestowed by the Holy Spirit can be one of two types: they can be new abilities that we did not previously possess and that He supernaturally downloads in us; or the Holy Spirit may put a "demand" on an existing talent to be used for God's glory by anointing and expanding it and taking it beyond what we could have humanly accomplished. In either instance, these gifts are all distributed for the purpose of ministry or service. "A spiritual gift is given to each of us as a means of helping the entire church." (1 Corinthians 12:7, NLT).

Let me tell you about my young friend, Leah Tillema. Her story perfectly illustrates the way the Spirit of God supernaturally gifts us with something new and unlearned. At sixteen years old, Leah became a believer while attending her grandmother's Pentecostal church. The moment she received Christ as her Lord and Savior, she was baptized in the Holy Spirit with the evidence of speaking in tongues.

By eighteen years old, however, she allowed the experience to fade, and Leah went her own way when she met her future husband. At twenty, she was married with a child on the way and very far from the God of her teen years. But life was not good and neither was her marriage. Two-and-a-half years into the marriage, the relationship escalated to its worst peak, and she was ready to chuck it all—that is, until she had a vision of Jesus walking into the room. "It is my will that you walk in my power," the Lord said. She knew at that moment that He was calling her back to Himself, and she was more than happy to return to Him.

It was a six-month journey before Leah finally got free of all the demons and strongholds in her life, but she persevered, and the dynamics of her life changed for the better. She returned to church and found herself being drawn to praise and worship teams within the church ministry groups. She had never really been a singer but discovered that she actually could sing and really enjoyed it!

One day, while singing on the praise team of a women's Bible study, a download of rhyming words came to her. They seemed like the structure of a spiritual song, but one she had never previously heard. Having never written music, she was quite captivated by it. She longed to put some music to it but could play no instrument. Upon her return home that day, Leah spied the guitar she had bought for her husband several months before. She it picked up and began to strum. There were instructions that accompanied the instrument, demonstrating how to form four chords. She kept working at them until she became proficient enough to put a melody to the song she had written and accompany herself as she sang it.

Leah was agog and wanted to share her new song with someone. The following week, with guitar in hand, she sang and played her new song, "I Will Not Fear," for the group leader of the women's Bible study. The leader was enamored with the song as well and asked Leah to sing it that day in the meeting. As the music went out, it had a profound impact on the group. The glory of the Lord filled the room, breaking the heavens open. Many were propelled forward for prayer and were delivered from the stronghold of fear as she ministered in song.

This instance was a game changer and catapulted Leah into a new realm. More lyrics and melodies were birthed, and the idea to record the songs began to swarm her thoughts. She knew the Lord was prodding her to do this, but how could she accomplish it? She had no extra money to move forward, yet the notion would not relent.

Finally, as an act of sheer obedience and raw faith, Leah took the leap and called a local studio. She booked a recording session to take place in six weeks. As she hung up the phone, she chastised herself. *What are you thinking? You have no money! How are you going to pay for this?* But God was working out His plan. When He calls us to do something, He will make a way. We need not stress out but watch Him work. Leah was on a faith expedition, and the Lord was going to show Himself faithful. One of my favorite sayings is "we don't know God is faithful until we need Him to be faithful." We will never know His faithfulness until we are put in a situation where we have to trust Him to be faithful to us, and then He shows up and shows off His amazing power and glory. Leah was about to discover that.

She sheepishly decided to post on Facebook what she had done...and something outrageous happened. People began to send her money for her project! She hadn't asked, yet the Holy Spirit began to speak to her Facebook friends to invest in her. As the funds came in, she felt that she needed to tithe on every dollar. She gave 10 percent of every cent that was deposited, and the more she tithed, the more the money came in. By the time the six-week period was up, she had enough to pay for the recording time with eleven dollars left over! Leah has now cut two albums of her own original songs and is working on her third. She performs her songs and leads worship wherever the Father opens the doors.

This is the way spiritual gifts work. The Holy Spirit will endow us with abilities and skills that we were not taught nor were able to perform prior to our new birth in Jesus Christ. In Leah's case, she was gifted with the ability to sing, play an instrument, and write songs. Oh, and by the way, she now also plays keyboard—another spiritual gift that she was not humanly taught.

The Lord will call us to do tasks we do not know how to do, but if we are willing to say yes to His call, He will give us strategies from heaven and will equip us abundantly above all that we could ask or think to accomplish those tasks. Our part is to partner with Him and take the leap of faith. (For more information about Leah or to purchase her albums, go to https://store.cdbaby.com/cd/leahtillema.)

Talents as Spiritual Gifts

Talents can also be transformed into spiritual gifts. The Holy Spirit might put a call on a talent to be used for the glory of God. For example, I play the piano. My friend, Paula Foster, plays as well. She always felt the call of God compelling her to use her talent to play for the worship service in her church. That was her ultimate call, the commitment where she was gifted and appointed. I, on the other hand, never felt that way about playing piano. Have I played in church? Yes, when there was no one else available, but it was never a passion nor did it feel like it was my main call. For me, it was a secondary call, serving where needed but not ultimately appointed. Yet in the case of my friend, she felt it was her ministry and played for many years; and because of her faithfulness, her abilities and proficiency at the keyboard increased. The Spirit put a demand on her talent and anointed her to play for the greater good of the church, which then became one of her spiritual gifts. Even though I have the same talent, it never became a spiritual gift. I have been appointed differently in the Body of Christ and am called to perform a different function.

Just as our physical body is made up of diverse parts, each having a different function, so too is the Body of Christ made up of different parts with different functions. Each is important for the Body to operate properly, working together to accomplish all that the Father has mapped out for us to do. No function or gift is greater than the other, but all are of equal importance. Romans 12:3–6 (NIV) very aptly says, "For by the grace given me I say to every one of you: Do not think of yourself more highly than you ought, but rather think of yourself with sober judgment, in accordance with the measure of faith God has given you. Just as each of us has one body with many members, and these members do not all have the same function, so in Christ we who are many form one body, and each member belongs to all the others. We have different gifts, according to the grace given us."

Because we have been fashioned individually with different gifts and callings, we will find ourselves naturally gravitating to and having a passion for certain activities. It's by God's design.

Let's revisit the young woman mentioned at the beginning of the chapter who was searching for her giftings. In a mentoring session, I asked her, "What is your passion? What do you feel drawn to?"

She rather self-consciously replied, "I like to quilt and sew, but I feel guilty taking up time doing that, so I've laid it down. I miss it, though, and think about it often."

I thought for a moment, then ventured on. "Perhaps the Spirit of God wants to use that talent for His glory, turning it into a spiritual gift, and that's why you can't quit thinking about it." Her eyes lit up at the possibility. We then began to brainstorm ideas as to how she could use that ability to serve others for the glory of God. She left with a spring in her step and excitement in her heart at the thought of returning to her long-ignored love. Now she had a starting point.

What do you love to do? What excites you? When you see others operate in a certain way, does it grab your attention? Do you find yourself gravitating toward specific things to do? This could your starting point. Just as I was drawn to supernatural healings even as a child, you too have a lure toward something for which God wants to use you. Your interests will not exactly match anyone else's because, again, you are uniquely molded to fit in a precise cutout piece in the giant jigsaw puzzle of the Church. Only you can fit into that spot! Even if you are called to the same position as another, you will operate a little differently than others.

That's why we should never compare ourselves to others, never be jealous of another's calling or gift, and never try to cross lines of our calling. We need to "stay in our own lane." We would probably be uncomfortable and fail at someone else's call anyway, as we are not outfitted to carry it out. Focus on what the Holy Spirit has gifted you to do. Therein is where your success, joy, and sense of fulfillment will lie.

The Holy Spirit Determines Our Gifts

It is the Holy Spirit's decision as to what gifts He will bestow upon us. We read in 1 Corinthians 12:11 (NIV; emphasis added), "All these are the work of one and the same Spirit, and he gives them to each one, just as *he determines*." The New Living Translation expresses it like this: "He alone decides which gift each person should have." Thus, there is no plausible reason to yearn to be like someone else or mope over their abilities. Focus on what the Spirit has called you to do, and be the best you can be at it, and you will receive your heavenly reward one day because of your faithfulness to develop your gift and fulfill your ministry as the Spirit so deemed.

Doers, Not Just Hearers

Once we have identified our gifts, we are to put them into practice. In James 1:22, it states that we are to be doers of the Word, not hearers only. Knowing about something and actually doing it are two separate things. We can read about something, talk about it, watch someone else function in it, but until we do it ourselves, it does not belong to us.

There are principles or physical laws that are established on the earth. One such principle is the Law of Use, which basically states that the more we work at something, the more we will improve. It is the same in the Kingdom of God with our gifts. The more we put them to use, the more skillful we will become. Yes, we might be a little "wobbly" with them at first, but if we continue to work diligently at them and pray over them, there will be an increase and a maturity in the operation of them.

It is explained this way in Matthew 25:29 (NLT): "To those who use well what they are given, even more will be given and they will have an abundance." If we do not use what the Spirit has designated to us, however, we will bear no fruit. It is important to develop that which has been given us. On the other hand, if we are faithful in what is before us, the Lord will promote and reward us by moving us into higher levels. There is great blessing in obedience, but by the same token, there is consequence to disobedience.

As you will recall, the parable Jesus told in Matthew 25 is about a man who was leaving town and called his three servants together, distributing "talents" of money (worth over $1,000 in today's economy) to each of them to invest for him while he was gone. To the first, he gave five talents; to another, he gave two; and to the last, he gave one. The one who received five talents immediately put his money to work and doubled it. The second servant, who was given two talents, did the same and doubled the amount of his investment as well. However, the last servant, who was assigned one talent, did nothing with it; he dug a hole and hid it. When the master returned from his trip, he asked for an account from each servant as to what they had done with the talents they were given. The first proudly presented his ten talents to the master, and the master replied, "Well done, my good and faithful servant! You have been faithful in handling this small amount, so now I will give you many more responsibilities. Let's celebrate together!" (Matthew 25:21, NLT). The servant given two talents joyfully displayed his four talents to the master, and the master repeated the same praise to him as he did the first. However, when he came to his third servant, the servant had a totally different story. He handed back the one talent he had received from his master saying, "I was afraid I would lose your money, so I hid it in the earth and here it is." (Matthew 25:25, NLT). The master was angry and called his servant "wicked and lazy."

The Word says that the servant was afraid, but fear is not a viable excuse to not do what God has appointed us to do or to choose not to go where He has said to go. He's looking for obedience and faithfulness. More than likely, just like the third servant, we too will be a little frightened of anything God calls us to do that we deem to be uncharted territory. Anything new can be unsettling. That's a normal human response. The Lord knows we are human 'fraidy cats, but over and over throughout the Bible, He reassures that He will be with us. "Have I not commanded you? Be strong and courageous. Do not be terrified; do not be discouraged, for the Lord your God will be with you wherever you go." (Joshua 1:9, NIV).

We are to trust the Lord and depend on Him to help us accomplish all that He has commanded us to do. If we know and understand how something is to be done, then we don't need the Holy Spirit's help; we will lean on our own understanding. But then, we will not spiritually grow nor will our faith. There haven't been too many times that God has asked me to do something that I actually knew how to do. But once I have figured things out and can do them on my own, He inevitably moves me on to something new that I don't know how to do! Even if He should put a demand on a talent or skill that we already possess, it will have variations and challenges that will stretch us and take us out of our comfort zone. It is the way of God to mature and grow us in our faith. However, we are in good company. Many of the patriarchs of the Bible were afraid of their assignments as well, yet they pushed past their fear and obeyed the Word of the Lord in faith. I think of Gideon, Jeremiah, Elijah, and Peter (before the day of Pentecost). Even that great patriarch, Moses, tried to squirm out of standing before Pharaoh when commanded of the Lord to go.

We are not to pander to fear. We are to take courage and rely on the Lord no matter what others think or say, whether we think we can do it or not, whether we think we're too old or too young, or any other excuse we might try to drum up. Courage is not the absence of fear, but it is pushing past the fear. I love how actor John Wayne puts it: "Courage is being scared to death but saddling up anyway."

If we do not follow the leading of the Holy Spirit, we are in disobedience, which is sin as indicated in the parable of the talents. This is serious business with the Father, as it shows a lack of faith in Him on our part. But if we will kick our faith into gear, saddle up, and step out of our comfort zone, we can be certain that He will never leave us or forsake us and will provide all that we need. And amazingly, we'll be able to accomplish more than we ever thought we could do! If we take one step toward Him, we will find that we will hit solid ground. And just think, we will actually be doing what we were created to do! He promises to be with us every moment of every day, and at the end of our life's journey, we will hear Him say, "Well done, my good and faithful servant. Let's celebrate together!"

That's all well and good, you might say, but how can I do the will of the Father if I don't know how to recognize His voice when He speaks to me? That's the second question others have posed most often. If that's you and that question has been floating around in your mind, then read on!

CHAPTER 14

Recognizing the Voice of God

Several years ago, a friend was excitedly telling me about all of the things the Spirit of God was saying to her. As I listened to her ebullient chatter, I wondered why I didn't hear God's voice. I too was a believer; what was missing? I asked others how they knew when God was speaking, and I was given a plethora of answers, but they were all rather nebulous. They said things like "you just know" or "you know in your knower." Huh? What did *that* mean? It was at that point I realized that I had to experience His voice for myself, and I went on a personal trek of discovery to that end. Here is what I learned.

In the John 10 discourse about the Good Shepherd, Jesus uses the metaphor of the shepherd and the sheep. We read in verse 7 that Jesus says His sheep follow Him because they know his voice. The sheep pen in ancient times would house several flocks together overnight in a high pen where a watchman would stand guard keeping the sheep safe from any would-be predators. In the morning, each shepherd would position himself at the gate and call his sheep. Those of his flock would recognize his voice and follow him out. The rest stayed in the pen until they heard their own shepherd's voice calling.

Jesus was making the point that His flock would recognize His voice against others and would follow His lead in the same way. With that in mind, I made the assessment that it wasn't that He was not speaking to me; rather, it was that I wasn't listening. But how was I to listen? The answer became clear—it was through my time in prayer, Bible study and, yes, sometimes in fasting. But the one other ingredient was that I had to be on alert and listen for His voice.

Mostly, we prefer to do the talking. We have what I call a laundry list of wants and needs that we present before the Lord. Now, that's fine, and we are told in Luke 11:9 to ask; however, if we want Him to answer, then we need to listen to what God has to say!

My mother had a friend whom we shall call Barbara*. Barbara had a sister who talked incessantly. When this sister would call, Barbara would often lay the receiver down and go do something else while her sister rambled on. Every once in a while, Barbara would come back to the phone, say, "Uh-huh," as if she were listening, and then continue with whatever else she was doing. The sister never realized that Barbara wasn't on the other end because she was so caught up in whatever it was that she had to say! Sometimes I think that's how we are with God—just all caught up in what we have to say. And although, unlike Barbara, God is listening to us, we also need to be quiet before Him and be on alert to hear what He has to say in whatever way He chooses to say it.

We were created in God's image for communion and fellowship with Him. He is a communicator, and we have been made to communicate as well. Communication is a two-way street, however—speaking and listening. God speaks and hears, and we were made to do the same. That's what relationships are made of. What a sad state of affairs it would be if our spouses or best friends did all of the talking and we were only to listen, never having an opportunity to respond to what was being said. So too it is with our Heavenly Father. He wants to hear from us and then desires to respond. He's an up close and personal friend who loves us beyond measure and wants to have fellowship with us. He is not distant and impersonal.

Because the Lord is creative, He speaks to us in several different and creative ways. Below, we will discuss several of the more prevalent ways in which God communicates.

---

* Name changed.

The Still Small Voice

I believe that the conscience created within us is the first indication of God speaking to man. It is that innate voice that we hear in our innermost being that knows the difference between right and wrong, good and bad. We don't need a revelation of the basics of good and evil for it is built into our souls. However, beyond that, God will speak directly to us in what the Bible calls the "still, small voice."

In 1 Kings 19:12, Elijah was getting a lesson in recognizing the inner voice of the Lord. The passage makes a point that the voice of the Lord is not loud and obvious as in a strong wind, or an earthquake, or a fire, but states it is the still, small voice to which we must be attentive. The scripture continues, "And it was so, when Elijah heard it…" (1 Kings 19:13, KJV). This is probably the way the Lord most often speaks to us today. It's what we might call an impression. Some would say it's a feeling or having a deep sense of knowing. We just *know*. Others call it an inner witness down deep in our souls.

Or it can also be a soft whisper as if in our ear. If then it is a soft whisper, it stands to reason that we must be quiet to hear it. It is of utmost importance that we surround ourselves with an atmosphere of quietude to tune our spiritual ears to the whisper. Our lives are filled with noise and busyness that constantly vies for our attention, but if we are to hear the Holy Spirit speak, we must shut ourselves in with Him without the distractions. That doesn't necessarily mean we must be constantly on our knees and sequestered in our prayer closet, but being quiet before Him is the operative word here. It's important to keep the din around us to a minimum in case the Holy Spirit has something to say.

When God speaks, it is for purpose and reason. It's not to entertain us. And the more obedient we are to His will, the more we will hear from Him. Will there be mistakes made while learning to hear His voice? Perhaps. There might be times when we misinterpret what the Holy Spirit is saying or our own "voice" gets in the way, but it doesn't mean that we give up. The more we press in and spend time with Him and the more we demonstrate obedience to Him, the more we will hear from Him and will more readily be able to distinguish His voice.

The Audible Voice of God

Though it is not common to audibly hear God speak, there are those who have had that experience. I can only remember one time that I heard His audible voice for myself. He called my name and woke me up out of a dead sleep. I heard nothing else, but I recognized that it was Him calling me, and I went to prayer.

My daughter had an experience when she was in her teens. She was seeking God for an answer concerning whether she should stay in a certain situation or leave. Together as a family, we prayed, asking the Lord's will and direction for her life. Not long afterward, while getting dressed one morning, she came running into my room, eyes wide and face flushed.

"Mom," she cried. "I heard a voice while I was getting dressed. I was asking God what He wanted me to do—should I go or stay?" She continued breathlessly, "And I heard a loud voice say, 'Stay!' "

Well, that was a pretty direct answer, and in obedience, she stayed where she was until the Father later led her out into a new season.

When Jesus was baptized in the Jordan River, the Father's voice was very notably heard by others (Matthew 3:17) and again, on the Mount of Transfiguration a voice was heard. "…[A] bright cloud came over them, and a voice from the cloud said, 'This is my beloved Son, and I am fully pleased with him. Listen to him.' The disciples were terrified and fell face down on the ground" (Matthew 17:5–6, NLT). The disciples obviously heard the voice, for they were very frightened. Though it is unusual today to hear the audible voice of God, there is nothing that precludes us from still hearing Him in this way.

The Scriptures

The Word of God is alive! It is not just words on a page but is the living expression of God's heart. "For the word of God is living and active. Sharper than any double-edged sword, it penetrates even to dividing soul and spirit, joints and marrow; it judges the thoughts and attitudes of the heart" (Hebrews 4:12, NIV).

When we read the Word, we should accept it as God speaking directly to us, as it will judge our hearts and thoughts, convict, encourage, give hope, create faith, guide, and tell us how to live according to His precepts, all to help us navigate this world and prepare for the next. We refer to this Holy Spirit-inspired, general written Word of God as *logos* (logic). It is a Greek term meaning "word" or "the Word." In the first chapter of the Gospel of John, the *Logos* is identified as the Divine Expression or the *Incarnate Logos* (word), i.e., Jesus in the flesh. "In the beginning was the Word, and the Word was with God, and the Word was God" (John 1:1, KJV) He is the living Word!

There is also another term that speaks of a specific word, directed to our specific circumstances. That word is *rhema*. It too means "word," but it refers to an individual revelation or personal inspiration. So we can say that *logos* is the general Word of God while *rhema* is a specific word or message to us. Have you ever been reading your Bible when a specific scripture lights up to you like a neon sign, speaking directly to a situation in your life? That's *rhema*, the Lord speaking to you directly through His Word.

Circumstances and Opened and Closed Doors

There are times when the Spirit of God will speak by setting up circumstances to let us know His intentions. He will "set us up" to get us to where He wants us to be. We may or may not be conscious of that leading at the time, but looking in our rearview mirror, we will probably eventually be able to see the pattern of how we were linked up with key people or were led to a certain place at a certain time. There are times when I've wondered why I was led a certain way, only to find out later that it was part of the greater divine picture for my life. We need to trust the process in the way He leads, even when, at the time, it may make no sense to us, and we need to take advantage of opportunities that come our way, unless we hear Him say no.

One of my favorite passages of scripture is Proverbs 3:5–6 (NLT): "Trust in the Lord with all your heart; do not depend on your own understanding. Seek his will in all you do, and he will direct your paths."

Another way that He leads is by opening and closing doors. Revelation 3:7 tells us that He opens a door, and no one will be able to close it, and He closes a door, and none will be able to open it. If a door seems open before you, take a step in that direction and test the waters. If it closes, don't try to pound it open. Sometimes it may be closed because we need to wait for the Lord's timing. There may be alignments that have to be set up before we can walk through. Or sometimes, we personally just aren't yet quite ready to handle what's on the other side, and God still has some work to do in us in order to equip us before we can step in; or else it's just not His leading… period.

However, that doesn't mean we throw in the towel. Keep praying for His direction, and in the meantime, find something else to do until He opens the awaited door. He will use everything in our lives to prepare us, even if we can't see it that way at the time. We are told to "occupy" until He comes (Luke 19:13). That means we are to be busy in His Kingdom in one way or another, not waiting around until we get a full view of what He's doing.

Sometimes, the Lord will instruct us to take a step first before we see the door open. That's a step of faith. He may invite us to take that first step, which is usually the hardest, but some doors will never open unless we leap toward them first. We are co-laborers with God. He has His part, and we have ours. We work together as a team.

In Exodus 3, we see a very telling story of how the children of Israel were led across the Jordan River even when the waters were at flood stage. This was during the harvest season, when the banks swell to their highest levels and the river's current greatly accelerates. The name Jordan River was derived from the Hebrew word meaning "the descender" because of the force of its heavy currents and whirling rapids. God gave a directive to the priests who were carrying the Ark of the Covenant, to go ahead of the people and step into the river, and then the water would dam up and all would be able to walk across on dry land. The priests had to step out in faith first, believing God would do what He said, and that is exactly what happened. When their feet touched the swirling water, the water heaped up to one side, and the priests were able to walk on dry ground. They then stood in the middle of the river bed, and all of Israel crossed safely to the other side. Note that the water did not stop flowing until the priests, by faith, followed God's exact direction and stepped into the water first. It was only then that the water banked. This was a mighty miracle, but it would not have come to pass had the priests run from God's command.

In the same way, there are times when the Lord will require us to "step into the water first" before they will part. We will need to step out in faith before we see the doors open. The first step might be a phone call or a conversation with someone to start the process, believing that the Lord will be waiting for us on the other side of it ready to reveal our next step. We don't usually get the full picture all at once. More often than not, it's one step at a time. I believe the Lord works this way because, one, we may become overwhelmed by the big picture, and two, He is ever expanding our faith by our having to trust Him each step of the way. We are to walk by faith and not by sight, step by step.

Dreams

There are many accounts in the Bible of those who have had heaven-inspired dreams. I think of Jacob, Joseph, Pharaoh, Daniel, Pilate's wife and the list goes on. Why dreams? Simply put, when we are asleep, there are no distractions. The Father has our full attention! Not all dreams are God-given. Sometimes they're caused by too much pizza before bed! But I have noticed in my own life that I will remember the dreams that are important after I awake.

Some dreams require interpretations because they contain symbolism. Back in Genesis, we read about a young man named Joseph who had prophetic dreams. He saw the sun, moon, and eleven stars bowing down to him which, in fact, turned out to be his family paying him homage many years later when he had become the second-in-command over all of Egypt. He also had the God-given ability to interpret dreams. He interpreted dreams for the palace baker, Pharaoh's cupbearer, and for Pharaoh himself. Each of those dreams contained portents that represented future events, and each of those dreams came to pass just as he had accurately deciphered.

Other dreams are straightforward. They need no explanation and are readily understood. I have had dreams that required interpretation, but more often than not, my God-given dreams are pretty straightforward. Several years ago, I had a dream about a high school classmate by the name of Bonny. Bonny and I had attended school together from second grade to graduation. Once we entered high school, however, we drifted off, going in separate ways. She married her high school sweetheart, Sam Coffman, who was also from our class, and that was the last I knew about her.

My family moved from that area during my freshman year in college, and I lost track of Bonny. But fifteen years later, while Brad and I were living in the Midwest, I had a dream about Bonny. I was back in my hometown, walking in front of the local post office, and Bonny was approaching me accompanied by four children. I had no idea how many children Bonny had in reality, or if she had any at all, or even if she still lived there in town. When we reached one another, she grabbed my arm and said, "Linda, please pray for Sam. We are in trouble." At that point, I awoke but couldn't get the dream out of my mind, and I started a prayer vigil for her and Sam. The dream continued to stay with me throughout the morning. I wondered what it meant. With this still on my mind, I proceeded to get dressed for the day, and then the Lord spoke to me in that still small voice that, by now, I had learned to recognize. He prompted me to write Bonny a letter and tell her about the dream and that I was praying for her.

He went on, "Then, tell her that I love her, and I have heard her prayers." I reminded Him that I didn't know where she lived anymore. I didn't know if she had moved away or if she still lived in our little hometown. He replied to my questioning. "Mail it to her old homestead in care of her mother." Though I didn't remember the house number, I remembered the street name, and it being a small town, I knew the mailman would know the house and whether her mother still lived there.

So I took another shot to try to get out of the mandate. "But, Lord, I don't know if her mother still lives there."

His answer: "She does."

I tried another angle. "Anyway, Bonny might not understand. I don't know if they are Christians, and she might think I'm crazy. Or even worse, she might think I'm a fortuneteller or something."

He didn't even qualify that with an answer. All was silent.

I tried to do my Bible study afterward but couldn't concentrate. The dream danced around and around in my head.

Finally, I became resolute. I knew I would have no peace until I complied. I grabbed a pen and a sheet of stationery, praying that the Holy Spirit would guide my hand as to what exactly He wanted me to write. As I put the pen onto the notepaper, the words began to transfer easily. I wrote that I hoped she remembered me. I told her about the dream and exactly what the Father had said. I stated that I was a Christian and was praying for them and to please not think I was a psychic or anything in that vein!

I sighed as I licked the envelope and placed it in the mailbox for pickup, comforting myself with the fact that I at least was obedient to do as He asked. We lived several states away anyhow, and I'd probably never see her again. I tried to cavalierly shake off my dread. Let her think what she wants; I don't care...but I did. In one way, I wanted her to respond, but in another way, I preferred not to hear back lest she call me a kook! Days turned into weeks and weeks to months, and I received no correspondence from her but did continue to pray for them.

After four months had passed, a letter appeared in my mailbox, postmarked from my old hometown. I sent up a quick prayer and, with a slightly elevated heartbeat, sat down and braced myself for the reply.

"Dear Linda," it began. "First, let me thank you for your letter…" Okay, that was a good start. The further I read, the more jubilant I became. Yes, at the time she received my letter, she and her four children were living with her mother in the home of her growing-up years. Sam was working a temporary job and living elsewhere due to the fact that he could not find employment in the area. It was not a good situation on so many levels, being separated for such an extended period of time, and they were getting discouraged. However, not long after my letter had arrived, Sam got a call for a job in the local area. Within that four-month timeframe, Sam moved home, started his new job, and they were able to move into a home of their own near to her mom. But more than that, Bonny went on to write, "Your prayers for us were very timely…We are both saved and depend on the Lord for everything in our lives." I was overjoyed! God knew what He was doing. He just needed a vessel to carry His message. Tears splashed without restraint onto the lined notepaper before me. I was so humbled that He called on me to encourage a sister in Christ and was ecstatic that I had overcome my self-consciousness and self-protection. The seemingly ridiculous heaven-request brought a powerful and on-time resolve to their difficult situation.

I'm always amazed at the ever-abounding love of God toward us and how He will go to endless lengths to assure us that we are in His hands. He does not forget or forsake His children. He will reach across state lines, or sometimes even around the world, to let us know that very thing.

Visions

Visions are different than dreams in that we are fully awake when we receive them. A vision is a supernatural overlay that supersedes the natural world. It's as if a movie screen from another dimension comes before us and plays out God's intentions.

There are two types of visions: open visions and closed visions. The open vision is when we are fully awake and our natural eyes are enabled to see into the supernatural dimension. As in dreams, these visions may be symbolic or straightforward. Nonetheless, these too are the Holy Spirit speaking to us, giving spiritual revelation and insight.

A closed vision is "seeing" a picture in our minds or in what we might call our inner spirit. We see it with our spiritual eyes rather than our physical eyes. It is more difficult to discern whether these are of ourselves or of the Spirit. It takes prayer and experience to be able to know the difference. However, if we continue to pay attention when God communicates in this way, we will more readily recognize this type of vision when it manifests.

Some people have dreams and visions more often than others. The dreams and visions are designated giftings that fall under the category of supernatural gifts of the Spirit, which will be discuss more extensively in Chapter 18.

The Voice of Others

I can't tell you how many times I've left a church service and said to my husband, "Is that pastor reading my mail? That sermon had to have been just for me!" Well, I'm sure there were others who benefited from the message, but I find it fascinating when a sermon addresses a situation that I'm dealing with or inspires heavenly guidance, especially when the pastor has no knowledge of my dilemmas!

The Lord Jesus will use others to confirm His leading. I love when something I've been hearing in my own spirit is confirmed by another who had no knowledge of what I was hearing. God will use anointed preaching to authenticate His word, but we might also receive a personal word from one who operates in the gift of prophecy, or the gift of word of knowledge, or word of wisdom to confirm. (This will be addressed further in Chapter 18.) We can actively seek a confirmation of God's will, for the Word does say that, "In the mouth of two or three witnesses shall every word be established" (2 Corinthians 13:1, KJV). I highly recommend that you beseech the Lord to validate a specific word to you. It will give you peace knowing that you are on the right path and are not being led astray by your own thoughts or by opposing voices.

A word of caution here: if you receive a personal prophetic word from someone, and you have not heard this word in your own spirit, do not rush into anything without inquiring of the Lord to reveal and confirm it to you directly. That well-meaning person could have missed the mind of God. If it is truth, it will speak in due season. Write it down in a journal, pray over it, and wait until you receive the Spirit's leading for yourself. Don't live by other people's prophecies. I tell you the truth, if in fact it's a true word from God, He will confirm it in additional ways, and it will come to pass!

Pop Culture

There may be some of you who will scoff at the idea that God can speak through secular pop culture, and, frankly, a few years ago, I would have agreed with you, that is, until I experienced it for myself. The Lord God Almighty is the Creator of all things, including all talents and all abilities. All were created for His glory, though some may pervert what they have been given, but He can use anything or anyone He so chooses to point us in the direction of His will.

Not long ago, a friend of mine described a problem that she was facing and prayed for some guidance. To her utter surprise, not long after, she was watching a secular television drama when a scene came up, and it actually spoke to her situation and provided her with an answer. She was shocked, but why not? God is totally relevant. We need to take Him out of our own puny box of how we think He should move and be open to whatever way He decides is best.

I heard an evangelist once share a story of how God spoke to him through the title of a pop song. I must confess here that I was rather dubious about the matter. However, not but a few months afterward, I had an occasion to experience it myself.

A new opportunity had been presented to me to expand my ministry, which appeared to be the fulfillment of a prophecy that was spoken to me several years before. I expeditiously needed to make a decision concerning it, and I was musing over it in the car on the way to church one Sunday morning. I shut myself in with my own thoughts and inwardly prayed, "Lord, is this it? Is this opportunity the fulfillment of what has been prophesied to me over the years?" Brad was driving and had tuned in to a pop radio station, and immediately upon praying that prayer, the song "This Is It" by recording artist Kenny Loggins played on the radio. Astonished cannot adequately describe my reaction! As I listened to the lyrics, they perfectly addressed what was going on in my life. Once I had recovered from the initial shock, I diffidently thought that this perfectly timed astounding personal message might be the confirmation that I was seeking. The following day, I took a step toward the opportunity, and the door opened before me. Every detail fell into place. Indeed, this was it!

I'm sure Jesus and the angels had a joyous laugh at the look on my face when that song came up. But it was a good lesson in being open to however He chooses to get our attention. Sometimes, He's rather unorthodox in His approach by our way of thinking, but He will get His point across if we will keep ourselves zeroed in to Him. We have limited preconceived ideas of how we think He should move and act, but He often will, and usually does, surprise us if we'll let Him be God.

Peace

The last way that I want to mention in recognizing the voice of God is by experiencing His peace in the midst of a decision. When Jesus is directing our steps, we will have a settled, internal peace that will signal us that the message or direction is indeed from Him. In Isaiah 9:6, a prophecy of the coming Messiah, Jesus is called the Prince of Peace. He wants us to have peace in every aspect of our lives. On the other hand, Satan, the deceiver, will always try to lead us astray, but his way does not bring peace. He brings chaos and confusion, but Jesus calms and settles our spirits, clearing us of all fear and anxiety. I like the way the book of Colossians states it in the Amplified Bible, "Let the peace of Christ [the inner calm of one who walks daily with Him] be the controlling factor in your hearts [deciding and settling questions that arise]. To this peace indeed you were called as members in one body [of believers]." (Colossians 3:15, AMP).

If we do not have peace when making a decision, then wisdom says to wait. We should not act without God's peace. If you are troubled within, then stop. That troubling will keep you out of trouble! There can be false peace in the excitement of a moment, but give things time to settle and allow true peace—the peace of God that passes all understanding—to manifest. If it does not, leave it in the dust and move on!

***

One might say that this all just sounds like pure coincidence. If that's true, then I have to believe God sets up our "coincidences." Nowhere in the Bible does the word coincidence appear. We are told in Psalm 37:23, Proverbs 16:9, Isaiah 26:7, and in so many other passages, that the Lord directs the steps of the righteous. We are not flung out into this world to flail aimlessly on our own. God loves us too much for that. However, if we choose to make decisions on our own without seeking His counsel, He will let us do so. He is not a tyrant or dictator, and we aren't robots. We were created with the ability to choose, but why would we prefer to chance it on our own when God's ways and plans for our lives are perfect and will continuously provide directions for the journey.

CHAPTER 15

The Serving Gifts

There are twenty-five Holy Spirit-enabled gifts that can be tracked in God's Word. These are broken down into three categories: the serving gifts (or motivational gifts, as some call them): the five-fold ministry gifts; and the nine supernatural gifts. These gifts are distributed for what Paul calls the "common good" or for the good of all (1 Corinthians 12:7).

Under the serving gifts category, we find eleven gifts listed mainly in Romans 12, 1 Corinthians 12, and 1 Peter 4. These gifts are to serve others and to meet the practical needs and functions of the Church. Perhaps you might readily identify yourself in some of these definitions as we explore each one.

Gift of Helps

We find the gift of helps mentioned in 1 Corinthians 12:28 (NAS): "And God has appointed in the church...helps..." Those who possess this gift prefer to come alongside another's ministry to provide support. They do not want a role of leadership but will throw in their abilities behind ministry leaders to help them meet their goals and calling. The gift of helps is earmarked by a preference for the routine, a keen eye for details, and a high efficiency to bring projects to completion. People with this gift choose to consistently remain with one ministry rather than move around from one ministry to another. Possessing a servant's heart, those gifted with helps are usually humble and loyal to their ministry leader. A good example of someone with this gift would be an administrative assistant to a pastor or ministry leader or a teacher's aide to a Sunday school teacher.

Gift of Service

The gift of service differs from the gift of helps in that those with this gift prefer to serve others by performing various tasks in different ministries. They would rather engage in short-term projects and prefer the diversity of floating from one task to another to render their assistance wherever help is needed. Those with this gift will be the first ones to volunteer whenever there is a need for practical projects to aid others and fill in gaps. They have a servant's heart and are willing to carry out menial tasks that no one else is willing to do and often will gladly jump into a job without being asked. These individuals excel in remembering small details, prefer to stay in the background rather than take on a leadership role, and would rather take direction than give it. Because of their willingness to assist in whatever ways they can, it is difficult for them to turn down those who ask for help even if it imposes on their own personal schedule. Paul mentions the gift of service in Romans 12:7 (NLT): "If your gift is that of serving others, serve them well." We can find those with this gift perhaps folding bulletins or cooking for a funeral, among other practical and unobtrusive undertakings.

Gift of Mercy

Individuals with the gift of mercy champion the poor, lowly, and sick. They have an immediate empathy and an extra measure of compassion for those who are broken or are in distress and desire to come alongside and actively help relieve others' suffering in whatever way they can. They are personally very sensitive and "feel" what others feel. The word mercy comes from the Greek word *eleeo*, which means to "feel sympathy with the misery of another and especially sympathy manifested in an act." Often, we find those with this gifting working in community service, hospitals or in prison ministries in an effort to improve dire situations. We should all seek to show mercy, but those with the gifting will go above and beyond the norm. Mercy is referenced in Romans 12:6, 8 (NIV): "If a man's gift is... showing mercy, let him do it cheerfully."

Gift of Hospitality

I have seen the epitome of this gift operate in a gentleman in our church. This brother loves people and goes out of his way to be friendly to all who walk through the church doors. Everyone who encounters him makes comment about his unusual accommodating and welcoming spirit. That is the gift of hospitality—the divine desire to make others feel welcome in one's church and in one's home. Those who are downloaded with this gift are the first to greet strangers and have a God-given knack to make others immediately feel welcome. They also enjoy hosting people in their homes, inviting others in for meals and, if need be, will offer lodging. Those with the gift of hospitality will volunteer their homes for church gatherings or home Bible study groups and find pleasure in planning parties and events. They are the ultimate extroverts! In 1 Peter 4:9–10 (NIV) we read, "Offer hospitality to one another without grumbling. Each one should use whatever gift he has received to serve others, faithfully administering God's grace in its various forms."

Gift of Administration

Administrators tend to be perfectionists. That is a part of this gifting. They excel at working with numbers and details and have a strong sense of organization. They are efficient with managing information and finances and are great problem-solvers. Those with this gift understand what makes an organization function and have the ability to accomplish stated goals of a ministry. In general, they are more data-oriented than people-oriented. Every ministry should have someone on their team who is gifted in administration for organization purposes.

I had shared earlier that when I established the food pantry, I had a lady on my staff who was a whiz with numbers and managing data. She kept all records of the grants that we were awarded, the accounting of our funds, and the incoming and outgoing of our donated resources. I don't know what I would have done without her. She clearly had the gift of administration.

Those with this gift could serve as executive pastors, book-keepers or administrative assistants. We can find this gifting in 1 Corinthians 12:28 (NIV): "And in the church God has appointed... those with gifts of administration..."

The Gift of Leadership

Having the gift of leadership enables one the capability to moti-vate and direct people to work in harmony to accomplish set goals. Those with this gift are visionaries who are more concerned with the overall picture than with carrying out the details. They tend to be people-oriented and are effective delegators. Leaders are entrepre-neurial and are risk-takers who have a strong sense of destiny and direction. They are usually the ones who will initiate and direct new ministries or businesses for the furtherance of the Kingdom of God. As examples, we find leaders heading up Bible studies, establishing new church plants or taking the leadership of boards and commit-tees. Romans 12:8 (NLT) identifies this gift: "If God has given you leadership ability, take the responsibility seriously."

Gift of Creative Arts

The gift of creative arts conveys spiritual truth and messages through a variety of art forms for the benefit and enjoyment of others, all done for the glory of God. These creative gifts include communi-cation skills, such as the written and spoken word; filmmakers and visual arts; technical and computer skills; lighting and sound tech-nology; music in all forms, i.e., singing, playing an instrument, and writing music; and the performing arts, which involves drama and dance. Worship leaders and bands, book authors, actors, and dancers would all fall into this category. Miriam, Moses and Aaron's sister, had the gift of creative arts, as noted in Exodus 15:20–21 (NIV):

"Then Miriam, the prophetess, Aaron's sister, took a tambourine in her hand, and all the women followed her, with tambourines and dancing. Miriam sang to them…"

Gift of Artistry

This gift is the inspired ability to design and construct tangible items created in the mind and constructed with the hands that will communicate God's Word in visual, creative ways. It inspires others to consider the message of Christ from a different perspective. Those with this gift include painters, sketchers, graphic artists, seamstresses, gardeners, woodworkers, and any who produce something with their hands for the benefit of the Body of Christ.

In our church, we have a gifted lady who paints prophetically during our Sunday morning services. Her art connects to the scriptures, giving us a visual image to consider along with the Word. If you are compelled to craft something tangible with your hands for the glory of God, then you have the spiritual gift of artistry. In the Old Testament, we see Bezalel was bestowed with the gift of artistry. "Now the Lord spoke to Moses, saying, 'See, I have called by name Bezalel…I have filled him with the Spirit of God in wisdom, in understanding, in knowledge, and in all kinds of craftsmanship to make artistic designs…'" (Exodus 31:1–4, NAS).

Gift of Giving

The gift of giving will very often come as a gift-mix with the gift of mercy. This gift is the divine ability to generously contribute money and resources beyond the Biblical mandate of tithing to other ministries or to those persons who are in need. Givers seek opportunities to give, even if it be to their own personal detriment. They feel duty bound and drawn to those who are in need of financial help in any way. Giving affords them great joy and a sense of fulfillment.

Givers do not seek accolades but prefer to give anonymously, solely giving for the glory of God. They are the ones who will collect and supply goods for homeless shelters and who finance missionaries and adjunct ministries. They understand the scripture in Romans 12:6, 8 (NIV), which says, "If a man's gift is…contributing to the needs of others, let him give generously…" Though they are generous with others, those with this gift tend to be conservative with their own spending.

Gift of Exhortation

The gift of exhortation has also been referred to as the gift of counsel, as that is what it fundamentally is. Those who are empowered with this gift love to speak words of encouragement and comfort to others, will offer wise counsel and guidance and, if need be, will admonish those who need spiritual discipline. Their motivator is the Word of God and their own experiences to urge others into action who may be discouraged or wavering in their faith. You will often find that the exhorter has little patience for those who want to live superficial Christian lives. Their mission is to rally others to a deeper walk with the Lord and to assist in growth to maturity in Christ. Many with this gift choose Christian counseling or mentoring as their life's work. The referring scripture to this gift states, "You must teach these things and encourage your people to do them, correcting them when necessary. You have the authority to do this, so don't let anyone ignore you or disregard what you say" (Titus 2:15, NLT). The exhorter takes this commission seriously!

The Gift of Intercession

The intercessor has the ability to consistently pray for long periods of time on behalf of others and will experience more answers to prayer than most. They are highly sensitive to the leading of the Holy Spirit and will feel an urgency and burden to "stand in the gap" as a prayer warrior for others until they see the fruit of their prayers. Those with this gift carry a greater measure of faith than others, as well as a heavy anointing on their lives. They have an unusual understanding of their authority in Christ and know the power with which they have been entrusted. "The earnest prayer of a righteous person has great power and wonderful results" (James 5:16b, NLT). Intercessors often host home prayer groups and head ministry prayer teams.

I have intercessors on my team who hold up my ministry in prayer every day. It is absolutely essential if you have any type of ministry that you include intercessors on your team. They will bombard heaven and earth for you until they have prayed you through. I believe they are the critical difference between the success and failure of a ministry. Don't leave home without one!

***

There are those who might add a couple of other spiritual gifts to the list. I personally am not so sure that I would classify them as such. One is the gift of celibacy, another is the gift of poverty, and another is martyrdom. I will leave those to your own conclusions, but the more important point here is that we identify our own gifts and be committed to developing them to further the Gospel.

CHAPTER 16

Five-Fold Ministry Gifts

In Ephesians 4:11–13 (NAS), we find a listing of what we refer to as the five-fold ministry gifts needed for the equipping of the saints and to build up the Body of Christ. Those with these gifts are given the responsibility by the Spirit of God to help equip believers to do the work of the Kingdom and to grow others to maturity in their faith. "And He gave some as apostles, and some as prophets, and some as evangelists, and some as pastors and teachers, for the equipping of the saints for the work of service, to the building up of the body of Christ; until we all attain to the unity of the faith, and of the knowledge of the Son of God, to a mature man, to the measure of the stature which belongs to the fullness of Christ." In other words, He wants His children to grow and be equipped to do Kingdom work on earth. Those with the five-fold ministry gifts are commissioned to help within this process through teaching, discipling, and training.

These five-fold ministry gifts can be offices or positions held in Church government. However, it is important to note that even though someone has the ministry gift, it doesn't always mean that he/she occupies the office. We will see, as we go through each one of these gifts, that the office holds a higher call, which means that you can operate in the gift without being called to the office, but you can't hold the office if you don't manifest that specific gift. Those whose gifts operate at an entry level could grow into the office, but not necessarily. Let's take a look.

Apostleship

In its purest form, the term apostle in the New Testament means "sent one." Once Jesus ascended to heaven and the Holy Spirit descended to earth at Pentecost, the disciples were given a promotion from disciples to apostles. They had been trained and mentored by Jesus Himself, equipped with power by the Holy Spirit and were now ready to be sent out as apostles to make more disciples by training, mentoring, and equipping as they had been taught. Jesus commissioned them to "therefore go and make disciples of all nations, baptizing them in the name of the Father and of the Son and of the Holy Spirit…" (Matthew 28:19, NIV).

Apostles today are still commissioned to develop and launch other members in the church body into their God-assigned ministries. They enjoy the process of bringing others to maturity in Christ through development and training. Additionally, some will plant churches. These can be either domestic churches or in foreign lands, ministering cross-culturally.

Those called to the Office of Apostle have a higher calling, operating at a more advanced level of leadership and occupy a position in Church government. They are anointed to develop and oversee pastors, churches, and ministries, and they display unusual wisdom in spiritual matters. They are usually ordained into their position, which is a commissioning and affirming by the laying on of hands by church elders and are officially recognized in the office.

Prophet

To prophesy means "to speak for another." The prophets in the Old Testament were uniquely appointed to speak for God as His mouthpiece to Israel, bringing messages of repentance and reform, warning and judgment, and future events. They were also called seers because of their ability to "see" into the spiritual realm. However, since the day of Pentecost, when the Holy Spirit came to earth with His gifts, the gift of prophecy has become available to all believers, not just a few specified prophets. But with this shift, there came differences.

Those with the gift of prophecy today do not necessarily stand in the Office of Prophet, as did the Old Testament prophets. All prophets will prophesy, but not all who prophesy are prophets. Those who are called to the Office of Prophet will hold a position of governance in the Church. Not only will they have a strong ability to prophesy, but unlike those with the simple gift of prophecy, which will edify, exhort, or comfort, they will have the divinely inspired capability of foretelling future events, as did the prophets of old. Prophets, well recognized for their gifting, will operate on a higher level of accuracy of supernatural messages and will consistently operate in other revelatory gifts through dreams, visions, and strong impressions. The prophet will have a wide measure of notoriety and a wider prophetic reach. More will be discussed in Chapter 18 concerning those with the simple gift of prophecy verses the Office of Prophet.

Evangelism

The gift of evangelism is the ability to effectively communicate the Gospel to unbelievers and lead them to a personal relationship with Jesus Christ. They are specifically anointed for this task and, as a result, will have a greater success rate than others in winning the lost. Those with this gift have an unusual boldness to share the Good News and possess an uncanny ability to be able to easily direct a conversation toward Christ. They carry a heavy burden for the lost and prefer being out in the marketplace with those who need to hear the message than within the four walls of a church.

The Office of the Evangelist is again a governance position in the Church. In addition to having all the attributes of the gift of evangelism, those holding the Office of Evangelist are officially and publicly recognized as such and will make it a career choice. The evangelist is appointed by the Spirit of God to travel to the nations to preach the Gospel and will witness multitudes coming to the knowledge of Jesus Christ.

I know a young man who is very readily identified as having the gift of evangelism. He shares his testimony everywhere he goes and, remarkably, is able to easily win others to Jesus, but he does not lead crusades. This is not his career calling, but he does these things in addition to his secular job, sharing the salvation message everywhere he goes. Therefore, he has the gift of evangelism but does not occupy the Office of the Evangelist.

What about the rest of us? Are we to lead souls to Christ or do we just leave it to the ones who have the gift? We are all told by Jesus in His Word to go into the world and preach the Gospel. Your world may not be across the planet but it might be your family, or your neighborhood, or your workplace. We all have a "world" where we are commissioned to share the Good News, and Jesus promised that His Word would not return void. Therefore, we are all called to be witnesses of His saving grace. We may not see droves of people come to Christ, but remember that Jesus went after that one lost sheep, and we need to go after that one, as well, in our own world.

Pastor/Shepherd

Those who are empowered to be a pastor/shepherd have the responsibility to oversee a local body of believers in a long-term relationship to assist with their growth and maturity in the Lord. In the New Testament, the Greek word for pastor—*poimen*—is actually translated as "shepherd." This same Greek term is used of Jesus, the ultimate Shepherd, in Hebrews 13:20 and as the Great Shepherd and Good Shepherd in John 10:2. Those called to be pastors are usually people-oriented and desire to train, equip, disciple, and involve themselves in the spiritual maturing of their local flock. A pastor can also be one who oversees an auxiliary ministry within the church or a small home group. They are charged in 1 Peter 5:2 (NLT) to "Care for the flock of God entrusted to you. Watch over it willingly, not grudgingly—not for what you will get out of it, but because you are eager to serve God."

The Office of Pastor, however, is an ordained position in Church government, and those who fill that office are publicly acknowledged in that position usually making it a career choice. Inherent in this gift is the enablement to preach, teach, counsel, and mentor. This would include senior/lead pastors as well as staff and associate pastors.

Encompassed within this group is also the missionary. Missionaries have a burden to bring the message of Christ to those in a foreign country or a second culture. Missionaries can also be associated with other professions, such as nurses, doctors, and teachers, adapting their skills in other cultures through the special work of the Holy Spirit, having the opportunity to share the Gospel through these avenues. Some countries do not allow the Gospel to be openly preached and, therefore, will bar the obvious pastor from coming into the country; but medical or teaching skills are often desperately needed, and these skills will readily open doors that might otherwise be locked.

Teaching

The teaching gift comes in many levels. There are those who are called to teach toddlers, some who prefer to teach teens and on up to adults. Some are called to teach on specific subjects, but all are part of the equipping of the saints. Those who teach have the ability to research and communicate spiritual truths and impart these truths clearly and systematically to others to bring understanding and motivation. They have a love for God's Word and diligently study to unearth the hidden things and are meticulous about the accuracy of their information. Teachers may be pastors, Bible study teachers or Sunday school teachers.

There's a warning to teachers, however, in James 3:1 (NLT). They will be judged more strictly by God because of their influence on others. It is not a position to be taken lightly. "Dear brothers and sisters, not many of you should become teachers in the church, for we who teach will be judged by God with greater strictness."

There are also those who are called to the Office of Teacher. These can be well-known Bible teachers with a public platform or those who are recognized and confirmed within the local church body, having extensive Bible-teaching experience. I think of Joyce

Meyer and other well-known Bible teachers when I think of the Office of Teacher. However, there are others in the local church who are anointed Bible teachers and are recognized and well-respected by the pastor and congregation for their gift, who have a major impact on people's lives. I would place them, too, in the category of the Office of Teacher.

***

Regardless of the level of operation, all of the five-fold ministry gifts are necessary within the Body of Christ to equip, raise up, and launch the saints into their specific callings. Can you move up into these offices? Yes, but though not all will be called to this level, the Lord wants to see all of us grow. Therefore, be diligent in your gift, be faithful to operate in it wherever and whenever the Lord opens the door to you, and then ask the Holy Spirit for the upgrade. Jesus said, "Ask and it will be given to you; seek and you will find; knock and the door will be opened to you" (Matthew 7:7, NIV).

CHAPTER 17

Introduction to the Supernatural Gifts

I love the supernatural gifts of the Spirit. Even as a child they fascinated me, but I don't think that's unusual. After all, we were all created with a supernatural soul, and we are, therefore, drawn to the "otherworldly." Wherever I minister, I see people who are hungry for the mystical. We desire to experience something bigger than ourselves.

Unfortunately, the spiritual gifts have come under unmerited controversy, and, sadly, it's the Church that has been the greatest critic. As with the baptism in the Holy Spirit, some say the spiritual gifts are not for today but ceased with the first-century church; some say they are overly stressed in the Charismatic/Pentecostal churches, and there's a lack of balance between the Word and the gifts, and others say they are flat-out of the devil. Thus, we have an anemic Church with no power and no authority, as very little emphasis is placed on the power of the Holy Spirit.

The gifts are our inheritance as children of the Most High God. Of the two billion Christians in the world today (the largest religious group on the earth), only approximately one quarter are Charismatic/Pentecostals according to the Pew Research Center.[6] If we would all come together under the Holy Spirit's power, we would shake the

---

[6] *Pew Forum* on Religion and Public Life (December 19, 2011), *Global Christianity: A Report on the Size and Distribution of the World's Christian Population*, p.67. See also *The New International Dictionary,* "Part II, Global Statistics: A Massive Worldwide Phenomenon."

heavens and the earth for the Kingdom of God and transform the entire planet!

Going out and proclaiming the Gospel message without the power of God behind us was neither what Jesus taught nor intended. Jesus Himself told His disciples after His resurrection to "go into all the world and preach the good news to all creation. Whoever believes and is baptized will be saved, but whoever does not believe will be condemned. And these signs will accompany those who believe: In my name they will drive out demons; they will speak in new tongues; they will pick up snakes with their hands; and when they drink deadly poison, it will not hurt them at all; they will place their hands on sick people, and they will get well" (Mark 16:15–18, NIV).

The apostles took that to heart, and after they were endued with this power from on high, they went out preaching the Gospel everywhere, with signs and wonders manifesting following the Word. "The apostles performed many miraculous signs and wonders among the people" (Acts 5:12a, NIV). As a result, the miracles drew crowds, and many believed in the Lord Jesus Christ, adding daily to their numbers. Paul wrote to the church in Corinth, saying, "My message and my preaching were not with wise and persuasive words, but with a demonstration of the Spirit's power, so that your faith might not rest on men's wisdom, but on God's power" (1 Corinthians 2:4–5, NIV). We need to back up the great claims we make in our preaching yet today by performing demonstrations that follow and confirm the truth of our words. The ministry of Jesus Christ followed this design as well—preach the Gospel, and confirm it with signs and wonders.

Signs are for the unbeliever to attract them to the wonder-working Savior. Telling unbelievers something about their lives that only God could reveal or healing their incurable sickness will immediately get their attention, and they will be much more open to the Gospel. If the American Church would allow the signs and wonders to operate in their services, it would bring life by the Spirit and act as a magnet to attract the unsaved. It was this Holy Spirit power show that filled up the auditoriums of Kathryn Kuhlman and the tents of Oral Roberts, A. A. Allen and others during the Voice of Healing Revival in the '50s and '60s. People are desperate for hope,

hope for their seemingly impossible situations. When comments are made that these gifts are not for today, it takes all hope away for the longing, despairing soul.

Precious Friends, please know this—there is *still* hope in Jesus Christ our Lord! Jesus is the same yesterday, today and forever (Hebrews 13:8). His Word does not change. He is *still* doing great things through His human vessels by the work of the Holy Spirit through us. Not only can we operate in the same power that Jesus did while on earth, but He promised that we would do even greater things. "I tell you the truth, anyone who has faith in me will do what I have been doing. He will do even greater things than these, because I am going to the Father" (John 14:12, NIV). Believe it, receive it, walk in it daily, and be His hands extended to others.

As we approach the coming end of days revival, I believe we will see the greatest spiritual harvest of souls ever experienced on earth, and those droves of hungry souls will be engaged by outrageous workings of the Holy Spirit. As the Spirit shows up, stadiums will fill up as we have never seen before. Not only will we see these manifestations appear in supersized assemblies, we, the "ordinaries" will be the ones equipped to perform those same signs, wonders, and miracles on the streets, in the marketplace, in our neighborhoods, in the local church, in our homes, in our workplace, and anywhere else we might be at the time. By all worldly accounts, Jesus was an "ordinary." He was born in a barn, lived in a small Judean town, and was raised by a carpenter. However, when the Holy Spirit came upon Him at His baptism, He became an "extraordinary." And because He returned to the Father and sent His Holy Spirit to all believers on the day of Pentecost, we too are called to become "extraordinaries." When the breath of the Godhead power breathes upon us (*pneuma* in the Greek and *ruah* in the Hebrew), we will, henceforth, be filled with the power to do all that Jesus did and greater. He wants us out in the world to become the work of His hands, changing others' lives, doing all and more than He did on earth.

Reasons for the Supernatural Gifts of the Spirit

The reasons for the gifts of the Spirit are: (1) to manifest or demonstrate God's power on earth; (2) to convince the unbeliever of God's existence; (3) to strengthen the faith and spiritual walk of the believer; and (4) to gain the interest and attention of all people to ultimately bring glory to Jesus. Jesus said, concerning His miracles, "Believe me when I say that I am in the Father and the Father is in me; or at least believe on the evidence of the miracles themselves" (John 14:11, NIV).

When He does the impossible in our lives, it gives us a testimony to share with others of what God has done and builds the faith of those who hear. The root word for testimony in the Hebrew means "do it again." So basically what is being put out into the atmosphere when we give testimony of the miraculous hand of God in our lives is, "God, you did it for me. Do it again for others." And it will create an interest in others who will clamor, "I want the same!" A personal testimony is powerful. It evokes hope and faith. We don't need to be eloquent of speech; we just give glory to our wonder-working God. When my mother was healed of a brain tumor (see the full testimony in Section 3), many people told us that her testimony gave them hope for their situations. Even when they would just see her walk into church, they were reminded of God's undeniable healing power, and it caused them to grab on to their own faith a little tighter. She was a walking billboard for the amazing power of God. Those kinds of miracles will edify and bring growth and development to the believers.

Gifts for All

All Spirit-filled believers have access to the nine supernatural gifts of the Spirit, and on various occasions, we may all operate in all nine of them. However, certain gifts will operate in some people more consistently. That is their main gift, and it will be recognized as such by others. We won't have to go around telling everyone how God uses us. It will be evident in the consistency of the works. I have, at one time or another, operated in all nine of these gifts, but I don't consistently operate in all of them. Therefore, I cannot say all of these gifts are my main gifts, but the ones that I do function in are recognized by others and are confirmed in the outcome of the works. That said, however, if the circumstances arise that I need the operation of a certain gift at that moment, I ask the Holy Spirit to manifest it in me for the good of the one to whom I am ministering for that specific occasion.

Now, we can, and should, ask the Spirit for a supernatural gift that we long to consistently have operating in our lives. As a matter of fact, we are even told in 1 Corinthians 14:1 to earnestly desire spiritual gifts.

We can also ask the Holy Spirit to increase our gifts, bringing them to a higher level of operation, and we can ask for additional gifts. Keep asking, keep seeking, and keep knocking. But we must understand that, ultimately, it is the Holy Spirit's fundamental decision, as we read in 1 Corinthians 12:11. Much has to do with the motives of our heart, the desperation of our desire to be used by Him and where He specifically needs us.

Do we need to be baptized in the Holy Spirit to be vessels for these supernatural gifts? Yes and no. There might be a lower level of operation in some of the gifts, but notice in the book of Acts, however, that the apostles didn't operate in that full power until they were baptized with the Holy Spirit's fire. And Jesus indicated to them to not leave Jerusalem but "wait for the promise of the Father" so they would be empowered by the Spirit to operate in the same gifts and same power as He. Through the Spirit of God, Jesus transferred that same authority to us. So why would you only want a "small piece of the pie?" When we become followers of Christ there is a vast storehouse of power-filled opportunities that await us. Salvation is stepping through the door, but there's so much more available in the Kingdom life beyond that.

CHAPTER 18

The Nine Supernatural
Gifts of the Spirit

The nine supernatural gifts of the Spirit are recorded in 1 Corinthians 12:8–10 (KJV): "For to one is given by the Spirit the word of wisdom; to another the word of knowledge by the same Spirit; to another faith by the same Spirit; to another the gifts of healing by the same Spirit; to another the working of miracles; to another prophecy; to another discerning of spirits; to another divers kinds of tongues; to another the interpretation of tongues…"

It is these gifts that produce the signs, wonders, and miracles through the work of the Holy Spirit. The astounding thing is that God has delegated us, His children, to perform these supernatural works! And He just hands them over to us out of His love for us and for the love of others. A gift is something voluntarily given to honor someone without expecting remuneration of any kind. I find it amazing that the Lord Jesus would entrust us with the power and authority to perform all the works that He did during His earthly life. There is no greater high in my books than seeing someone cast aside their wheelchair or crutches and walk or toss their oxygen tanks and breathe on their own, healed by the power of God. I'll take the Holy Spirit show over any of the greatest shows on earth!

Gifts Grouped Into Three Categories

The nine supernatural gifts are categorized in three specific groups according to their workings. The first group is the revelation gifts. Those gifts listed under this category are: the gift of word of wisdom, the gift of word of knowledge, and the discerning of spirits. They are grouped together as such due to the fact that they all have the element of supernatural revelation. They each reveal unknown information inspired by the Holy Spirit through our thoughts. We can say then that they operate in the mental realm.

The second group is the power gifts, which are: the gift of faith, gifts of healing, and working of miracles. These gifts manifest in the physical realm through the mighty power of the Holy Spirit to execute impossible works, circumventing established operations in the natural.

The last group is the utterance gifts. These operate in the spiritual realm and include: the gift of prophecy, the gift of tongues, and the gift of interpretation. They are the speaking gifts bringing God's messages to earth.

The interesting thing about all of these gifts is that, although they are uniquely and specifically separate, they will often overlap and work in tandem with one another. An example of that would be having supernatural knowledge that someone has a certain illness, and then, through the gifts of healing that illness is supernaturally eradicated. Another example would be discerning an evil spirit that is causing a hindrance to a prayer and then receiving a breakthrough miracle through the gift of working of miracles once the evil spirit is cast out.

Revelation Gifts—Word of Wisdom

The gift of the word of wisdom is just that, a *word* of wisdom, not *all* wisdom. Obviously, only God is all-knowing and all-wise, but He will reveal a fragment of His wisdom to us when needed for specific situations through a mental impression, dream, vision, etc. Therefore, this gift is a God-given specific plan for specific circumstances in a specific moment. Those who operate in this gift will be able to give supernatural wise counsel for direction, instruction, advice, and problem-solving under the unction of the Holy Spirit. We can ask the Lord ourselves for wisdom in our circumstances, and I trust that we all do so rather than only going to those with the gift of word of wisdom. God wants to hear from us too, but we can also go to someone with the gift to confirm what we have heard. If I have a major decision to make in my life, I pray for God's wisdom, but I will also ask one who operates in that gift for discernment as to what he/she is hearing from the Lord as well.

A good biblical example of receiving a word of wisdom is the story of Joseph as told in Genesis 41. Not only did Joseph interpret Pharaoh's dream about seven years of a coming crop abundance followed by seven years of famine, but he was also able to offer a wise, God-impressed solution to the problem, which was to store crop reserves during the years of plenty for distribution in the lean years. This was the operation of a word of wisdom. And of course, we know that Pharaoh recognized the standout wisdom of Joseph and put him in charge of the project. God set Joseph apart from the rest by giving him a heavenly plan. The word of wisdom will bring solutions to problems that those in the secular world don't have the ability to solve. It will set us apart as well as give us the advantage and will bring glory and attention to God.

We all need wisdom on occasions in our lives. It would be wise of all of us to ask for wisdom! "If you need wisdom—if you want to know what God wants you to do—ask him, and he will gladly tell you. He will not resent your asking." (James 1:5, NLT). But we can also ask the one who has the word of wisdom gift for some help!

Revelation Gifts—Word of Knowledge

Like the gift of the word of wisdom, the word of knowledge is not all knowledge of all things but, rather, is a portion of information supernaturally inspired by the Spirit of God. It is a measure of revelation given to an individual for a specific occasion or particular reason to more effectively minister. Jeremiah 33:3 (NAS) says that God will reveal the secret and hidden things: "Call to me and I will answer you and I will tell you great and mighty things which you do not know."

The word of knowledge reveals information about the past or the present in someone's life or in circumstances. Those operating in this gift will either "see" things in the supernatural realm through revelatory dreams or visions or will "hear" things through impressions or an inner voice. Jesus accurately knew (impression or inner voice) the details of the Samaritan woman's past and present life (John 4:17–18) and He saw (vision, dream, or mind's eye) Nathanael through the Spirit sitting under the fig tree (John 1:48).

In the Old Testament, Elisha knew the location of the army of the king of Aram who was at war with Israel. This was a word of knowledge. Time and again, he would reveal to the king of Israel the location of Aram's campsite and would foil Aram's evil plot. This enraged the king of Aram, and he called his officers together demanding to know which one of them was the snitch. Their answer always gives me a good chuckle. " 'None of us, my lord the king,' said one of his officers, 'but Elisha, the prophet who is in Israel, tells the king of Israel the very words you speak in your bedroom' " (2 Kings 6:12, NIV). Jehovah, the Revealing One, was whispering the secret things in Elisha's ear. He continues to do that still today for His kids.

One more time, let me impress that it is crucial to know the voice of the Holy Spirit. Had Elisha not discerned His voice, he could not have forewarned the king of Israel. We cannot operate in these gifts unless we recognize when the Spirit of God is speaking and accurately interpret what He is saying.

I had an incidence a few years ago that led to a veteran's healing. One Saturday afternoon, I heard the Spirit of the Lord say two words, "Hiatal hernia." I didn't have a hiatal hernia nor did I know anyone else who did, so I recognized that it was a word of knowledge. I asked the Lord to show me who it was.

While in church the next day, I asked the Spirit to point out who had the hernia, but nobody was highlighted to me either in the morning or evening service. Did I hear wrong? Did I make it up? I was puzzled.

That week, a friend of mine who headed up a veterans' ministry, called and asked if I would come to their monthly meeting to pray over the needs. I was no longer thinking about the hiatal hernia when we met that evening. When it was prayer time, the leader of the group asked if there were any prayer requests. Several raised their hands, but a visitor sitting in the back of the room stood up. He was clearly distraught. "I need prayer," he said. "I have had a hiatal hernia for several weeks and am in misery. I can't eat and can hardly drink anything. I've lost twenty-five pounds, and there doesn't seem to be any help in sight. So I'm asking God to heal me or kill me (seriously, he said that) because I just can't take it anymore."

I immediately stood up and pointed to him. "I have been looking for you!" I explained about the word of knowledge that I had received. The young gentleman was astounded that God loved him so much that He would disclose his dire situation to a stranger.

I laid hands on the area of the hernia and had the group surround him, all agreeing with me in faith. We prayed believing that this was his night for a miracle. As we were petitioning the Lord, the young man said he could feel heat in his midsection. Then, flush with excitement, he raised his hands in praise with unbridled tears sliding down his cheeks and declared that he knew he was healed!

Following the service, a potluck was served, and to prove out his healing, he ate a serving of every dish set out, including the chocolate cake! A few weeks later, he returned to give testimony of the miraculous healing touch of God. He affirmed that he had no more pain and was now gaining his weight back. What a mighty God we serve! Friends, the Spirit of God will give us the advantage of knowing the hidden and secret things.

In January of 2005, I had an experience in my own life when I needed a Holy Spirit heads-up in a financial situation. We had invested a good sum of money in a fairly new company. We personally knew the president, and he would call us on a consistent basis to keep us informed of the company's activities and progress. Suddenly, his calls ceased, and when I tried to contact him, the calls were not returned. I became quite concerned, and after trying to call one more time, decided I needed some Holy Spirit insight.

I committed to fasting and prayer and went off to a quiet place with Bible in hand to hear God's voice. I asked the Lord to show me something in the scriptures that would give me some understanding for the situation. I felt impressed to turn to Isaiah 36 and 37. I had no idea what this passage was regarding but turned to it anyway. It is the account of Sennacherib, king of Assyria, warring against the walled cities of Judah during King Hezekiah's reign. The plan was to takeover Judah, but Jehovah intervened and Sennacherib was unsuccessful. As I read this, I saw the word "takeover" like a flashing neon sign light up in my mind's eye, and the Lord exposed the reason why we were not getting any calls back. I just knew the company was in the midst of an unfriendly *takeover*, and the president did not want us to know.

The next day, the president's assistant, Josh*, called to let us know that we would be getting a phone call from the president shortly. Josh was a believer, so I took the opportunity to question him about what I heard the Lord say. He hesitated a bit and then said he would have to call me back and hurriedly hung up.

Josh did call me back later that day. He said that he had to get clearance from the president to divulge the information I had requested. Yes, there was a company trying to take them over! It was not friendly, and he asked that I would pray. He confessed that when I told him about that word of knowledge I had received, he "almost fell down and had to hold on to the wall" to hold himself up! Eventually, our prayers were answered, and the deal was routed. "For everything that is hidden or secret will eventually be brought to light and made plain to all" (Luke 8:17, NLT).

God loves us and showers His gifts upon us by the Holy Spirit as His expression of love toward us. They are the benefits of serving the One True God.

---

* Name changed.

Revelation Gifts—Discerning of Spirits

As we rapidly approach the rule of the antichrist, I believe the gift of discerning of spirits is one of the most crucial and vital gifts needed by all Christians. Jesus warned us that in the last days, "False Christs and false prophets will appear and perform great signs and miracles to deceive even the elect—if that were possible" (Matthew 24:24, NIV). It is this gifting that will give us the ability to see and hear into the spirit world in order to identify the source of operation behind a behavior or supernatural manifestation—whether it be the spirit of God, the spirit of man (the work of the flesh), or the spirit of Satan. To discern means to "perceive or distinguish."

The spirit of God could be the Holy Spirit, but it could also include God's holy emissaries, His angels, carrying out God's will. These spirits only work for our good.

There is also the work of the flesh, or human spirit, which is the tendency to do good or evil depending on how the flesh is influenced.

The third type of spirit is the satanic spirit. These spirits are only about doing evil. Satan's work is done by principalities, powers, rulers of the darkness, and wicked spirits in high places (Ephesians 6:12).

Satan is not a creator; he is created by the Great Creator and can only imitate what God does, thus he deceives by doing counterfeit supernatural signs and wonders.

There is a story in the book of Acts about a time when Paul and Silas were met by a slave girl who "had a spirit by which she predicted the future." She followed them around, shouting, "These men are servants of the Most High God, who are telling you the way to be saved" (Acts 16:17, NIV). Well, that sounds pretty legitimate, doesn't it? However, this went on for days, the Bible says, and Paul finally had enough of the harassment and cast that spirit out of her. It sounded like she was saying something good, but Paul discerned it as a harassing evil spirit, not the Spirit of God. It was annoying and clamoring. That is not God's way. The girl was immediately set free.

This is why we are told to test the spirits. 1 John 4:1 (NIV) admonishes, "Dear friends, do not believe every spirit, but test the spirits to see whether they are from God, because many false prophets have gone out into the world." How do we test the spirits? First John 4:2–3 (NIV) goes on to tell us, "This is how you can recognize the Spirit of God: Every spirit that acknowledges that Jesus Christ has come in the flesh is from God, but every spirit that does not acknowledge Jesus is not from God. This is the spirit of the antichrist, which you have heard is coming and even now is already in the world."

It is of the utmost importance that we understand this so that we are not easily deceived. The occult is surfacing more and more and will do so the closer we get to that last trumpet call. Many will follow the New Age gods of this world because of the deceptive power they see through the counterfeit manifestations, but it will lead to their destruction.

The manifestations of the evil one include fortune telling, extra-sensory perception (ESP), tarot cards, crystal balls, crystals, palm reading, tealeaf reading, Ouija boards (no, it's not a game!), soothsaying, voodoo, black and white magic (they are the same—both are evil), séances, divining rods, astrology in all forms including horoscope reading, psychic readers, and I'll also throw in this new game the kids are playing online—Charlie Charlie. If you have any apparatuses, books, magazines, games, videos or anything that smacks of the occult in your home, get rid of them! I can't stress this enough! I have had way too many people asking for deliverance—Christians included—who tell me they have demonic activity in their homes only to find that they are lodging some of these cultic objects on their shelves. The devil is cunning and tries to get into our lives in any way that he can. The Apostle Paul said that Satan masquerades as an angel of light. Many are oblivious to this fact. The Word of God warns us to have nothing to do with these things: "Let no one be found among you who sacrifices his son or daughter in the fire, who practices divination or sorcery, interprets omens, engages in witchcraft, or casts spells, or who is a medium or a spiritist or who consults the dead. Anyone who does these things is detestable to the Lord…" (Deuteronomy 18:10–12, NIV)

We are spiritual beings made in God's image. The center of our being is the spirit, and it's the spirit that communicates with God. Therefore, by God's design, we hunger for the spiritual realm and the supernatural. Satan is only too happy to oblige because the Church has failed to feed that supernatural desire by teaching on the Holy Spirit and His gifts and giving place to the Holy Spirit in our services. If the Church at large would acknowledge and allow the operations of the Spirit of God, we would not have the rush toward the occult that we have today. We would be providing the real thing.

As Spirit-filled believers, we not only have the ability to identify evils spirits, but we also have been given the power and authority to cast them out. (Luke 10:19) Much of Jesus's public ministry recorded in the Gospels involved sending evil spirits packing and setting their victims free. The apostles did the same. And today we, too, have that same authority and power to do as such. In Mark 16:17, Jesus testifies to the fact that this sign—casting out demons—will accompany those who believe. We don't have to be afraid of demons; they are afraid of us because we are carriers of the power and authority of God. Demons know that when we use the name of Jesus, it activates the Holy Spirit's power in us, and they have to flee. I read something not long ago that really hit home with me. The writer stated that he wanted to be the kind of Christian that when he enters a room, the demons jump out of the windows! That should be the prayer of all of us: let God arise in us and His enemies be scattered straight out the windows. All glory be to God!

Power Gifts—Gift of Faith

Faith—a small word with a big impact. Jesus said that even if we only have enough faith the size of a mustard seed, we can move mountains and uproot mulberry trees. It is the very basis of our Christian doctrine and belief. When we get saved, it is by faith. We believe what we cannot see with our physical eyes or hear with our physical ears, yet we know that our Savior, Jesus Christ, has forgiven our sins and has made us a new creation in Him. The evidence is our changed lives—how we now think, act, and what we put our focus on. Though we may not have seen the Lord or physically heard His voice or viewed heaven in the natural, yet we have an inner witness (the Holy Spirit) assuring us that Jesus is alive, and He will do exactly what He said He would do. Jesus said, "Blessed are those who haven't seen me and believed me anyway" (John 20:29, NLT).

Therefore, if we have put our trust in Jesus for salvation, we have a measure of faith. But there is also a deeper, more abiding faith where we continuously trust God for all of our needs and know He's going to come through for us in every situation. Quoting from the New Living Translation of Hebrew 11:1, faith is "the confident assurance that what we hope for is going to happen. It is the evidence of things we cannot yet see." As Christians, we need to be faith-powered. If God said it, that should settle it.

Here's how it works. Proverbs 18:21 tells us that life and death are in the power of the tongue. We are to speak life into our circumstances by speaking what God Almighty speaks. It is by faith that we speak out what it is that we believe. Releasing faith-filled words and quoting the scriptures with our voice gives it substance, which is our confidence in the truth of His Word.

When God speaks in whatever way He chooses, we are to believe it and declare it into the atmosphere by faith thus giving it substance. Faith empowers the presence of God to break through the line between the spiritual and the physical realm. By speaking what is heard in the spiritual and believing in our hearts, we are walking it over the bridge of faith to manifest into the natural.

Additionally, we must also put "feet to our faith." We believe in our hearts, but we then must move in faith. James 2:26 (KJV) states, "Faith without works is dead." Faith is an action word. It is active, not passive. We do all that we can do, and then we stand and let the Lord do what He is going to do. We partner with God. We declare what we hear in the spiritual and then take action in what we can do. I have prayed for those on walkers and in wheelchairs to be healed, and then I tell them to put action to their faith by standing up and walking in the name of Jesus.

Now those with the gift of faith, a highly elevated level of trusting God, are uniquely empowered by the Holy Spirit with a greater capacity to believe for the impossible. Regardless of what is heard or seen in the natural realm, they will pay no heed if it is contrary to what God has said.

The gift of faith is the very foundation that puts all of the other supernatural gifts into action. Without this type of immovable, unshakeable, unwavering faith, the manifestations of signs, wonders, and miracles will not come to pass. Faith generates power. It is the activator. It produces the power by which the Holy Spirit works.

Throughout the Gospels, we see many miracles performed because of someone's faith. In Matthew 9:29, Jesus said to the two blind men who were healed that it was their faith that made them whole. The woman with the issue of blood was healed because she believed if she just touched the hem of Jesus' garment, her health would be restored (Mark 5:34). A father's faith in Jesus brought his daughter back to life (Matthew 9:18). We read in Luke 7:9 of a Roman centurion's slave made well because of the centurion's belief in the Messiah. The Canaanite woman's daughter was set free of demons because of her mother's faith (Mathew 15:28). As you can see, in each of these accounts, someone had to believe.

Conversely, Mark 6:5 states that Jesus could not do any mighty miracles in his hometown of Nazareth because of the people's "unbelief." He was only able to heal a few sick but couldn't do the mighty miracles as He was able to do in many of the other cities. In this case, I believe that the hatred and jealousy toward Jesus blocked His being able to do those other phenomenal works. In general, the townspeople wanted nothing to do with Him or His power to do the miraculous. However, there must have been some who were open to Him because he did heal a few sick. Faith, with an expectancy that what we ask for is going to come to pass, is crucial if we want to see the greater works. Again, whether it be the one praying or the one receiving, or both, someone needs to activate their faith and be open to the work of the Holy Spirit.

Power Gifts—Gifts of Healing

The gifts of healing are the supernatural enablement to cure sickness and diseases for the body, mind, and spirit, separate from medical science or natural means. It is by the miraculous work of the Holy Spirit through the name of Jesus.

Ninety percent of Jesus's recorded ministry was spent healing the sick. He then passed that on to His followers after His ascension. We have been mandated to lay hands on the sick and have been promised that they shall recover (Mark 16:17). This is a sign that follows those who believe. Healing and faith go hand in hand. We can't have healing without someone exercising faith. It has been said that "prayer without expectancy is unbelief in disguise." When we pray for healing, we must expect that what we request is going to happen. Jesus said, "If you believe, you will receive whatever you ask for in prayer" (Matthew 21:22, NLT). Sometimes, it happens immediately; sometimes, it's over a period of time, but our faith must not vacillate.

Healing was part of the atonement, the work of Calvary. Isaiah 53:5 (KJV; emphasis added) states, "But he was wounded for our transgressions, he was bruised for our iniquities: The chastisement of our peace was upon him; and with his stripes *we are healed.*" Notice that it states we *are* healed. That means present, ongoing, for today!

This is the only supernatural gift that is plural—the gifts of healing. Though the scripture doesn't necessarily address why it is plural, from my own experience, I believe it is because there are specialty healings, similar to the way that medical providers specialize. I have observed that certain people who have this gifting also "specialize" in certain types of healings. Just as with the other spiritual gifts, no one gets everything. We are to function as a body, and each of us has been given our own special and unique place and purpose. This is reiterated in 1 Corinthians 12:27–31 (NIV): "Now you are the body of Christ, and each one of you is a part of it. And in the church God has appointed first of all apostles, second prophets, third teachers, then workers of miracles, also those having gifts of healing, those able to help others, those with gifts of administration, and those speaking in different kinds of tongues. Are all apostles? Are all prophets? Are all teachers? Do all work miracles? Do all have gifts of healing? Do all speak in tongues? Do all interpret? But eagerly desire the greater gifts."

Often those who operate in the gifts of healing will also be gifted in the word of knowledge. The Spirit of God will reveal an illness in someone's body or the root of an illness. There are also times when the gift of discerning of spirits will expose an evil spirit hindering a healing, such as, a spirit of infirmity. These gifts working in tandem are extremely helpful to more effectively minister.

We have seen over the years that there were those who have had mega healing ministries, such as Kathryn Kuhlman, Oral Roberts, Smith Wigglesworth, to name a few. But in the next revival wave, we will see untold numbers of people rise up with the anointing to pray for the sick. They will go out into the streets and marketplace, laying hands on those with illnesses and diseases, witnessing their recovery in Jesus's name. They will not have a personal agenda or a major public ministry nor will they be necessarily known by the masses. They will just be the ones who will answer the call of the Spirit to be a last days Kingdom harvester.

Power Gifts—Working of Miracles

The working of miracles is the divine intervention in or a temporary suspension of, the regular operation of the laws of nature and physics by the working power of the Holy Spirit. There are natural laws that were put into place when God created the earth. One of those is the Law of Gravity. When we drop an object, it freely falls to the ground, pulled down by the force of gravity. That's the Law of Gravity in operation. It would be a miracle, however, if we dropped an object, and it free floated in the air without any earthly intervention, thus circumventing the Law of Gravity. Miracles display the supremacy and magnificence of the Godhead by backing up the truth of the Word. They are signs and wonders for the unbeliever to prove the existence of God and for the believer, they give a testimony to share and build faith.

We see many miracles documented in the Old Testament. Moses parted the Red Sea when God told Him to lift up his rod and stretch out his hand. That obviously was an intervention in the regular operation of nature. It was the working of a miracle. Elisha, the prophet, caused an axe head to float. Meshach, Shadrach, and Abednego were thrown into a hot, fiery furnace and walked out of it perfectly whole and unsinged. And there are several more examples. We also see miracles in the New Testament by the hand of Jesus, and then in the early Church in the book of Acts. Jesus turned water into wine, raised Lazarus from the dead, and fed 5,000 people with only five loaves of bread and two fish. The apostles carried on the working of the miraculous. Two examples of this would be (1) Peter striking Elymas the sorcerer blind for a season and (2) Peter's supernatural escape from prison by an angel.

Throughout the ages, there have continued to be miracle workers, and yes, we are still experiencing miracles in this generation—on-the-spot supernatural weight loss, amputated arms and legs growing back, the raising of the dead, gold dust and authentic gems appearing in services, and much more.

I prayed for a lady who had several disintegrated vertebral discs. She was in constant pain and had to use a walker to help her move around. This had gone on for many years with no medical cure available. After we prayed, she began to walk without assistance, testifying that the pain had disappeared. She was from another state, and when she returned home, made an appointment with her doctor. She declared herself healed to the doctor. So he ordered an X-ray to see just what was going on. To his utter amazement and bewilderment, the disintegrated discs were regenerating themselves. This is impossible in the natural realm—vertebral discs do not regenerate themselves. The doctor was a Buddhist and this sister, as a believer, had been witnessing to him throughout the years with no apparent impact. However, upon seeing this miracle before his very eyes and knowing how the body works, he was much more open and attentive to hear as she told him about her miracle-working God. Rather than these being unusual, they are soon going to be the new norm in the last revival wave. These signs will follow those who believe!

Utterance Gifts—Gift of Prophecy

The utterance gifts, which are prophecy, tongues, and interpretation, are the gifts that notably characterized the Pentecostal movement over the years. To prophesy is the supernatural ability given to designated individuals to speak a message from the heart of God to the Church for the benefit of the believers. 1 Corinthians 14:22 (NAS) explains that "…prophecy is for a sign, not to unbelievers but to those who believe." As I mentioned in the earlier section on prophecy, in the Greek language, to prophesy means to "speak for another." We could say that those gifted this way become God's spokespersons. In the Hebrew language, the word prophecy indicates a "flowing forth or springing forth." It does feel that way when a word is given, like a bubbling up and flowing out of one's inner spirit.

Under the unction of the Holy Spirit, prophecies are spoken in the known language of the messenger and listeners so that all may understand. It can be in a corporate church setting or for a personal, one-on-one prophetic message. Simple prophecy is for edification (to build up, strengthen, uplift, encourage), exhortation (to counsel, admonish, urge) or comfort (to console, reassure, speak peace), as told in 1 Corinthians 14:3. We call this forth-telling, which could also include anointed preaching. However, the one who stands in the Office of Prophet will not only have the simple gift of prophecy but will additionally have the ability to foretell future events and will strongly operate in many of the other supernatural gifts. Thus, all prophets will prophesy, but not all who prophesy are prophets.

There was a major shift between the Old Testament prophets and the New Testament prophets when the Holy Spirit came at Pentecost. The Spirit of God would come upon the prophets of old when they received a prophetic word, but the Holy Spirit now dwells within, and prophecy has now become available to all Spirit-filled believers. We are told in 1 Corinthians 14:1 (and again in verse 39) that we are all to especially desire, covet, and be eager to prophesy.

Utterance Gifts—Gift of Tongues

Many have become confused with the difference between speaking in tongues and the gift of tongues. In order to have the gift of tongues, one must be able speak in tongues, but they are not one and the same.

Receiving the infilling of the Holy Spirit will be evidenced by speaking in tongues. The purpose of that personal prayer language is to edify ourselves—that is, to spiritually build ourselves up in the faith in worship and praise. "He who speaks in a tongue edifies himself" (1 Corinthians 14:4, NIV). It is also our direct prayer line to the throne room of God. When we don't know how to pray, the Spirit of God prays the perfect prayer through us (Romans 8:26–27).

The *gift of tongues*, however, is speaking in an unknown or unlearned language under the anointing of the Holy Spirit as a message to the Church or in a corporate assembly to edify the listening believers. But how can the Church be edified if we can't understand the language? The gift of tongues is paired up with the gift of interpretation, which we will unpack next. What's the point of the gift of tongues and interpretation, then, when we could go straight to prophecy? The answer lies in 1 Corinthians 14:22 (NAS), where Paul writes, "So then tongues are a sign, not to those who believe but to unbelievers." As prophecy is a sign for the believer, conveyed in the known tongue, so the gift of tongues is a sign to the unbeliever, delivered in an unknown tongue to confirm that God is in the house.

In Acts 2 on the day of Pentecost, it is said that those 120 people who gathered in an upper room of a house spoke in thirteen different languages. These were foreign languages to them, unknown and unlearned, but they were enabled to speak this way by the power of the Holy Spirit. However, when those who had gathered outside heard the 120 speaking in tongues, they understood what was being said because it was their native languages. This was a sign and a wonder. The Word says those who heard it were "confounded" and "amazed" and "marveled" because these tongue-talkers were uneducated and were speaking in foreign languages. There was no way they could have known how to speak those languages in their own ability.

Today, the gift of tongues is most often spoken in an unknown heavenly language rather than any unlearned earthly language. However, I know of cases where a message has been given in an unlearned language and was understood by someone in the meeting as their native tongue, verifying that the interpretation was correct.

Please know that the baptism in the Holy Spirit with the evidence of speaking in tongues is for *all* believers, but again, the gift of tongues is a separate upgrade of the gift for a public setting that is given by specified believers. In 1 Corinthians 12:28 (NIV; emphasis added), we read, "And in the church, God has *appointed*...those speaking in different kinds of tongues." Note the context. Paul is discussing spiritual gifts here, and it would, therefore, stand to reason that, within this context, he is speaking about the gift of tongues.

Utterance Gifts—Gift of Interpretation

If the gift of tongues is to edify the Church, it would do us no good if we didn't have an interpretation to know what the Spirit of God was saying to us. The gift of interpretation goes hand in hand with the gift of tongues. It is the supernatural, anointed telling of the unknown message in tongues, given in the known language of the hearers. Messages in tongues are dependent upon an interpreter and should not be given in a corporate setting unless there is one present who can interpret. If there is no other person in the meeting who can interpret, the Word says in 1 Corinthians 14:13 (NIV) that the one who gives the message should pray for the interpretation. The responsibility becomes theirs; otherwise, we are told in verse 28 that "if there is no interpreter, the speaker should keep quiet in the church and speak to himself and to God."

The gift of interpretation is just that—an interpretation or explanation. It is not a word-for-word translation. It is an overall understanding of the message. That's why some interpretations are longer than the tongues message or sometimes shorter.

Paul says in his letter to the Corinthians that it is better to prophesy than to speak in tongues unless there is an interpreter. The reason being that prophecy is spoken in the known language of the listeners, and they will immediately understand the given word. However, a message given in tongues along with interpretation will equal prophecy. Therefore, all that applies to prophecy will apply to tongues with an interpretation.

1 Corinthians 14 is called the *Robert's Rules of Order* for the execution of spiritual gifts. God is not a god of chaos and confusion. He is a god of order. If not handled properly, there can be disorder in the church in the way people operate in the gifts. Therefore, we are given the following guidelines for the operation of the gifts in public gatherings:

1. Messages in tongues, interpretations, or prophecies should be given one at a time. Each should wait his/her turn and not interrupt the other.

2. No more than three supernatural utterances should be given in a meeting. A tongue utterance, along with an interpretation, would be considered one message. So conceivably, there could be two tongues-and-interpretation messages plus a prophecy or vice versa within one service.

3. As mentioned before, in the case of the gift of tongues, an interpreter must be present or the one speaking out the tongues message should either interpret it himself/herself or remain silent and not speak out the message. The Spirit of God does not overtake our bodies and make us lose control. The ones who are given the message have control as to whether they speak or not and at what point they speak out their utterance. (1 Corinthians 14:27)

4. Prophecies and gift of tongues with interpretation are to be judged. In the Old Testament, the words of the prophets of God were not to be judged. They were sure. However, since the indwelling of the Holy Spirit is broadly given, we are told to evaluate the word for truth and accuracy. "Let two or three prophesy, and let the others evaluate what is said" (1 Corinthians 14:29, NLT).

Judging a Word of Prophecy

Here are some questions to ask when judging a prophetic word:

1. First and foremost, does it align with the scriptures? Anything contrary to the Word of God should be ignored. His spoken Word will always align with His written Word.
2. Does it bear witness in your own spirit? Ask the Lord for discernment. If something doesn't sit right with you, approach with caution.
3. If it is a simple prophecy, ask did it exhort, comfort, or edify? After a prophetic word, we should not feel discouraged or condemned. It should uplift, give hope, encourage, and comfort. Even if it is an admonishment, the Lord never beats us down.
4. If the word concerns a future event, did it come to pass? It may take a while to prove out, however, eventually it will speak if it's a true foretelling.

Yes, there are times when someone might have misinterpreted the true word. Does that make them a false prophet? No! The scriptures tell us that we see as if we are looking in a dim mirror. That's why we are told to judge the word—not the person giving the word—but the word itself. If you look throughout the Bible in both the Old and the New Testaments, false prophets received their messages from the dark side. They were not people of God nor were they serving God. Those who might make mistakes and miss what was said by the Holy Spirit are still followers of Christ. We are all learning to walk by faith and need to continually learn to discern the voice of the Spirit.

It makes me sad when churches "throw out the baby with the bath water" and squelch the move of the Spirit because perhaps someone got it wrong, and so the Holy Spirit is regulated to a side room (or out the back door). He needs to be the main event, not the side show! We are told not to quench the Spirit: "Do not stifle the Holy Spirit. Do not scoff at prophecies, but test everything that is said. Hold on to what is good" (1 Thessalonians 5:19–21, NLT).

Both pastors and congregations who work together in the gifts will see church growth and will reach their highest potential as a body.

Let us not ignore the Holy Spirit, but let us embrace Him and His gifts. Once we enter into the door of salvation through Jesus Christ, then let us continue to step into all the wonderful things God has for us through the power of the Holy Spirit. He wants to use *you!*

CHAPTER 19

Stepping into Your Destiny

My heart's greatest desire is that you identify the way God has gifted you and begin to pursue the destiny that He designed for you long before you were born. We were not called to be spectators on the bench of life but to get into the game and bring others to the knowledge of Jesus Christ. Jesus said in John 20:21 (NAS), "…as the Father has sent Me, I also send you." We have been commissioned to bring the Gospel to the world, using the gifts He has entrusted to us.

Outlined below are some practical steps for you to take in order to move into the center of God's will for your life, whether you have already found your track but are seeking more clarity or are just starting your expedition toward the discovery of your destiny.

First, I have created a Personal Spiritual Gifts Assessment that can be accessed online at www.itsbeginningtorain.com. I highly encourage you to take this assessment. It will give you a starting point and identify the gifts that you already possess. There, you will also find other tools to help you along the way. If you prefer a paper form, I also offer a separate workbook that contains the Personal Spiritual Gifts Assessment, the Fruit of the Spirit Self-Examination, and chapter worksheets that can be used in a classroom situation. (See the back of this book for more information.)

Once you have identified your gifts, begin to pray for guidance for God's specific plan and designated place of service assigned to you. Practice His presence through praise, worship, and tuning your heart toward Him. Learn to know His voice and become alert to the ways He speaks. Out of your intimate relationship with Him will flow the gifts. I would also recommend that you do some fasting, if you are able, along with prayer while in this season of seeking Him. Fasting will help to focus completely on Him and signal to Him that you mean business!

Thirdly, pursue the Holy Spirit to infill you with His power, giving you the evidence of speaking in tongues if you have not yet received this. We all need this power to be greater witnesses of the Good News and to enable us for service using His gifts just as Jesus did. Signs, wonders, and miracles will follow us in the same way.

1 Corinthians 4:20 (NIV) puts it like this: "For the kingdom of God is not a matter of talk but of power." We need to declare Jesus as Lord and Savior, but we also need the power behind us to demonstrate Him through the gifts of the Spirit.

Next, ask the Spirit to help you to fully embrace whatever gift-mix He has chosen for you. Whatever gifts they are, they will be perfect for you. Accept your assignment and become fully engaged, following His leading. We need to be willing, obedient, and flexible to do whatever He asks. He may ask us to do a hard thing. He may ask us to go beyond our comfort zone in order to step into His assignment. We need to be bold as lions for the Kingdom of God. Whatever He says to do, we must do it if we want to be used of Him. We need to sidestep fear and step out in faith. We need to take courage in His promises that He will be with us with every stride that we take. He promises that He will use us in ways we never imagined or dreamed possible. The Apostle Paul wrote to Timothy, "This is why I remind you to fan into flames the spiritual gift God gave you when I laid my hands on you" (2 Timothy 1:6, NLT).

Others may not understand when the Father asks us to do some "strange" thing. They may even think we are out of our minds, but He doesn't operate in the earthly way of doing things. His ways and thoughts are higher than ours, and if you want to be a world-changer for the Kingdom of God, He may ask you to do some unusual things too. There is a price to pay. Jesus says, "If any of you wants to be my follower, you must put aside your selfish ambition, shoulder your cross, and follow me" (Matthew 16:24, NLT). It may cost you everything—your plans, your hopes, your dreams—in exchange for His. Are you willing to pay the price? It will be worth it.

Also, it's imperative to stay busy doing Kingdom work. We are told that whatever our hands find to do, do it with all of our might (Ecclesiastes 9:10). Do something that you feel a nudge toward. We all have something inside us that draws us that was purposely put there by the Father. If you like to help others, volunteer in a food pantry. If you have a desire to pray for others, visit a hospital and lay hands on the sick. I can tell you that most people lying in a hospital bed would be glad for some prayer! Often, it has happened that what someone thought was an arbitrary decision to just go do something turned out to be exactly where the Spirit was leading them in the first place.

If you begin moving toward the supernatural gifts, I would suggest initially launching out and practicing your gifts in a small group, such as home cell gatherings or a Sunday school class. In this way, your faith will be built and confidence will be gained. Then the Lord will gradually advance you to larger platforms if you are faithful and obedient to the call. He doesn't want us to stay in one place and become stagnant. He wants us to continue to grow and mature in our gifts. One of the scriptures the Father gave me many years ago when I was first starting out was Habakkuk 2:3 (NLT):

> But these things I plan won't happen right away.
> Slowly, steadily, surely, the time approaches when
> the vision will be fulfilled. If it seems slow, wait
> patiently, for it will surely take place. It will not
> be delayed.

The call on my life has slowly, steadily, surely come to pass just as the Spirit disclosed to me all of those years ago in my vision. I'm sure there are some of you reading this who are waiting for the fulfillment of your promises, too, so let me encourage you that without a doubt, if it's a God-promise, it will certainly take place. Wait patiently and be faithful to the call before you. Do what He asks you to do, and in His time, your promise will be fulfilled.

And don't allow Satan or any naysayers steal your confidence in God with lies, accusations, and discouragements. No matter what you may have done in your past, it doesn't negate the call and purposes that God has for your life nor does it disqualify you. If you need to repent of some wrongdoing, then repent and get on with it. Don't stay down and fail to fulfill all that the Lord has planned for you. That call will remain on your life as long as you are on this planet.

Maybe you are thinking that you only occupy a small corner of this world, only having local influence and impact, but that's what this new revival will look like. It will be made up of many who have a short reach yet who will have a major effect on those who surround them, much like a rock thrown into a lake that generates ripples that push further out. What is important to realize is that all souls are the same, whether they are souls of those across the ocean in other nations or those in our household or backyard. We all have a sphere of influence assigned by God to reach out to others. In any event, souls are souls, and all are important to the Father. Jesus died for all. Some will cry out for the nations; others will cry out for their neighborhoods. Don't despise or dismiss the "local missionary" call. God will bless those who are called across the waters but will also bless in the same way those who are called across the street.

One last thing, between 1 Corinthians, chapters 12 and 14 (which concern the gifts) lies chapter 13, known as the Love Chapter. The scriptures were set up in this way to remind us that, even if we had all power and could operate in all of the gifts, love is still the greatest power on earth, and if we aren't motivated by love, we are only making a lot of meaningless noise. One day, we will no longer need the gifts, as Jesus will be the fulfillment of all. But love will last forever. Whatever we do, we must do in love.

> Love is patient and kind. Love is not jealous or boastful or proud or rude. Love does not demand its own way. Love is not irritable, and it keeps no record of when it has been wronged. It is never glad about injustice but rejoices whenever the

truth wins out. Love never gives up, never loses faith, is always hopeful and endures through every circumstance. (1 Corinthians 13:4–7, NLT)

Time is accelerating, and end time prophecies are being fulfilled more quickly than in any time in all of history, all whirling toward the return of the Messiah for His Bride, the Church. The massive unprecedented last days harvest will come just prior to His return. In the meantime, we have all been called to do His good will to bring in as many as possible into the Kingdom of God, and to that end, have all been fashioned by the work of His hands.

SECTION 3

The Miraculous Work of His Hands

For You, Oh Lord, have made me glad by what You have done; I will sing for joy at the works of Your hands.

—Psalm 92:4 (NAS)

CHAPTER 20

Angel Encounters

Do not forget to entertain strangers, for by so doing some people have entertained angels without knowing it.

—Hebrews 13:2 (NIV)

Angel in the Details

Tawny Triska Pollard

I heard my cell phone go off and looked at the caller ID. My heart sank. It was the school…again. I prayed a quick prayer. "Please, Lord, don't let it be the school nurse," but when I answered, my fears were unfortunately confirmed. Yes, my thirteen-year-old daughter, Tawny, was sick again, and they asked if I would please come to the school and pick her up.

It was a pattern that consistently occurred within the previous couple of months. She'd get a cold, the flu, a sinus infection, or something in that vein, and her pediatrician would order up more antibiotics, decongestants, antihistamines, and the like. She'd feel better, go back to school for a week, or sometimes just a few days, only to get sick again and need to come home. This time, it was an ear infection. Needless to say, I was worried but didn't know what to do. "God, what's wrong with my daughter? Please, give me wisdom and direction."

It was Monday, September 27, 1999, and I was working the front counter of our pet store in Laguna Beach, California. Mondays were usually light-traffic days in the store, and as there were no customers shopping at that moment, I immediately called the doctor's office to ask for an appointment for the umpteenth time.

While I was on the phone, a gentleman came in. I had never seen him before. This was a neighborhood shop, and we knew most of our clientele. He was quite tall, with light brown hair and light-colored eyes and looked to be in his early forties. Other than his height, he looked unremarkable.

He asked me in a whisper where he could find the cat food. I motioned toward the appropriate aisle and finished up my phone call. He returned to the counter with a small bag of the feline food. I hurriedly rang him up as I needed to leave pronto to pick Tawny up for her doctor appointment, but he seemed to want to linger and chat.

"That sounded like a doctor call," he remarked casually.

I did not want to be rude yet needed to be on my way and hastily answered, "Yes. My daughter is sick, and I have to pick her up from school." I hoped he'd take the hint that I was in somewhat of a rush, but he didn't seem to be affected by it at all.

"Oh, is she ill often?" he inquired. It seemed a strange question, but I found myself telling him of her repeated health issues.

Startlingly, he said, "Well, I'm a doctor. It sounds like she needs a certain type of blood test."

"Really? What kind of doctor are you?" Now he had my attention.

He simply said he was an internist.

My curiosity was piqued, so I probed further. "Where is your practice?"

He replied offhandedly, "Oh, that doesn't matter."

I asked his name and got the same response. "That doesn't matter. Now, if you give me a piece of paper, I'll write down the blood test she needs."

He scribbled something on a piece of scrap paper and said, "Here, give this to her pediatrician and insist that you want this blood work done."

With that, he left with his little bag of cat food tucked under his arm.

I called out to my husband, who was in the back of the store. Very briefly, I told him what had happened and handed him the fragment of paper.

"I'd like to meet him. Where is he?" Brad peered out the glass door into the parking lot.

"Why, he's right there..." My voice trailed off. There was no one in the parking lot nor were there any cars moving. I went outside to search for him, but he had vanished. There was no sign of him anywhere. It had been less than a minute when he left.

I was in wonderment of what had just happened but didn't have time to ponder it for long as I scurried out the back door.

We directly headed to the pediatrician's office. I handed the doctor the scrap of paper and insisted on that particular blood analysis. He conceded to do it, but I could tell he was a little put out by it. I surmised he didn't want his judgment second-guessed, but I was on a mission.

We immediately went to a lab to have the blood tests done. The couple of days' wait was difficult, but I pressed in to prayer. What would the results be? I held on to my faith and trusted the Lord for my daughter's healing, whatever the outcome.

Finally, the tests were in. The nurse on the other end of the phone line gave me the grim news: Tawny's red blood cell count was dangerously low, but they had pinpointed the problem—she had contracted mononucleosis. The antibiotics she was consistently being given only added to her already lowered immune system. I was stunned! That blood work was exactly what was needed for her diagnosis! The good news was she didn't have to be hospitalized. The bad news was that she would need complete bedrest. I secured a tutor during that time to help with her schoolwork, and we began the long and winding road of rebuilding her immune system. After three months, she had fully recuperated and was able to return to school.

I believe that God heard my desperate cry that day and sent an angel—His messenger—with the answer I needed. We never did see that "doctor" again, but I'm not surprised. I'm sure I entertained an angel unawares.

The Bible says that we sometimes interact with angels without knowing it (Hebrews 13:2). The word "angel" originated from the Greek word *angelos*, meaning "messenger." Accounts of angels are recorded throughout both the Old and New Testament in thirty-four of the sixty-six books of the Bible. We read of angel visitations to Elijah, Jacob, Daniel, Zacharias, Mary the mother of Jesus, Jesus himself…and the list goes on.

Angels are created beings, each with different rankings and assignments, all created to do God's bidding. Some of their tasks include worship, messages, announcements, warring, warnings, guarding and rescuing, and probably elements of things we will never know on this side of heaven. They appear either as readily recognizable celestial beings: "Suddenly an angel of the Lord appeared and a light shone in the cell. He struck Peter on the side and woke him up" (Acts 12:7, NIV), or they can manifest disguised as human beings: "The two angels arrived at Sodom in the evening…They called to Lot, "Where are the men who came to you tonight?" (Genesis 19:1, 5, NIV).

Angel sightings and ways in which they intersect our lives are still reported today as in my story above. In this next story, we see how the angel of the Lord rescued a mother and her three children from what had the potential of being a very dangerous situation.

Do You Believe in Angels?

Cindy Hufford-Stewart

Cindy Hufford Stewart and her husband, Dennis, were parents of three young children—two toddlers and a babe in arms. They lived in Glendale, Arizona, near Luke Air Force Base Hospital where Dennis worked, about a thirty-minute drive from their home.

With only one car between them, Cindy would often drive Dennis to and from work. On this particular November afternoon in 1973, she loaded the kids into the car and set out on Beardsley Road, a seldom used two-lane highway, to pick Dennis up as she had done so many times before. Though this route was less traveled, it was more direct than the alternative major thoroughfare and much more pleasant, with scenic cotton fields spreading out along both sides of the road.

It was all familiar and routine as she motored on with the happy chatter of her children behind her until the vehicle's panel lights began to flash. Gradually, the car decelerated and ultimately, as she carefully steered off the road, it stopped altogether. Though she tried to restart the engine, it was to no avail. Now what? She could stay in the car and hope for another vehicle to come by and drive them on to the base, but then again, there was no knowing how long it would take for someone to come along, not to mention the risk of riding with a stranger. The other option was to walk to the base, which was still quite a distance.

After she assessed her dilemma, Cindy decided on the latter, and with the baby in her arms and her toddlers in tow, she began her hike along the deserted highway, fervently praying God's protection over them.

Not long into their arduous trek, a large luxury automobile pulled up beside them, and the lone driver rolled down the window on the passenger's side. Funny, Cindy hadn't heard the sound of a motor come up from behind. She cautiously leaned down to look into the car and observed an unusually tall man with distinctive snow-white hair wearing a dark suit.

He simply asked, "Can I help you? I can take you wherever you need to go."

Cindy definitely needed the help, but did she dare get into the stranger's car with her three young children? There seemed no other alternative, and although badly frightened, the young mother and her brood climbed into the back seat. All of her senses were on alert as they took off down the highway.

The gentleman tried to put her at ease with casual conversation. "Do you believe in angels?" he asked as he looked into the rearview mirror.

Somewhat taken aback, Cindy replied in the affirmative, "Yes, I do." She thought it a rather odd question but didn't pay much attention to the rest of his prattle. She had one goal—get to her destination safely.

After what seemed to be an eternity, they finally pulled up to the military hospital without incident. The man stopped the car at the front curb to let them off, and the little band scrambled out. Cindy had left the car door open while she helped the children get organized onto the sidewalk with her back to the vehicle. She turned to close the door and thank the gentleman for his kindness, but to her astonishment, there was no one there! Strange. She hadn't heard the car door slam or the car drive away. She looked up and down the street where there was a clear view for several blocks…but nothing. The white-haired man and his luxury car had just disappeared.

In Psalm 34:7 (NLT), we read, "For the angel of the Lord guards all who fear him, and rescues them." They watch over us and protect us and guard our way, sometimes seen and sometimes unseen. As His children, we can trust God to take care of us through His angels. We don't have to be afraid or anxious about anything.

In a dream some years ago, an angel came to me to remind me of that very thing. I was concerned over some events that had transpired in my life. I tried not to give these things much heed but couldn't come above the stress. One night, with those worries on my mind, I fell into a troubled sleep, and an angel came to me in my dreams. This angel manifested as tiny sparkly particles that all came together and formed a being. I perceived the angel to be female. She had chin-length, wavy blond hair in the style of a 1920s movie star and wore a simple long white dress. She looked at me and said, "Be anxious for nothing. Be anxious for nothing. Be anxious for nothing," and then dissipated in the same way she had manifested.

When God repeats something three times, you know He means it! It referred to the scripture in Philippians 4:6–7 (NAS), "Be anxious for nothing, but in everything by prayer and supplication with thanksgiving let your requests be made known to God. And the peace of God, which surpasses all comprehension, will guard your hearts and minds in Christ Jesus." Angels do not say anything other than what God instructs them to say, so a message from an angelic being comes straight out of the throne room of God.

As this scripture states, we are to be anxious for nothing. Nothing means *nothing*—not our families, not our finances, not our jobs, not our sicknesses, not anything! We are to pray, trust Him, and rest in His peace, knowing that He will take care of whatever concerns us. Jesus too said in Matthew 6, in His famous Sermon on the Mount, that we are not to worry about anything for our heavenly Father knows what we need, and that's all we need to know!

Up from the Ashes

John Hodge

It was winter in the early 1960s, and from his classroom window at California State College in California, Pennsylvania, John Hodge could see the skies getting dark with snow-laden clouds. John's professor dismissed class early since a blizzard warning had just been announced. Though John only lived approximately thirty miles away, he was concerned about the road conditions, especially since it was his turn to drive the carpool that day, and he was responsible for getting everyone home safely.

The three carpool riders met at his parked car, and John hurriedly pulled out of the college parking lot as the snow flurries made their downward descent. Maybe he could beat the blizzard and get home before things got too severe. He prayed to that end and set out on his way.

Though John negotiated the roads as well as possible, the weather began to deteriorate quickly making it harder and harder to keep the car steady. Icy snow pelted down on the wings of heavy winds, filling up the vehicle windshield and the highway underneath. Drivers were losing control of their vehicles and slipping and sliding off the roads and, in some cases, into one other. The road crews had yet to show up with hot ashes to help with the situation.

John held tightly to his steering wheel and prayed that the Lord would give him safe passage, but his car too began to slide sideways when he hit an icy patch on Coal Center Road. His vehicle slid uncontrollably down a snow-covered embankment. There the car sat, embedded in the snow, with no apparent recourse for rescue. Though none of them were hurt, how were they going to dig themselves out?

As the young students discussed their options, an older-model pickup truck suddenly appeared behind them, driven by an older man dressed like a coal miner. He emerged from the vehicle and rummaged through his truck bed, retrieving a bucket of ashes and a shovel. There was nothing distinguishing about the man, and he said not a word to the boys but set to work shoveling the hot ashes around the entrenched car tires. John slowly accelerated the car as the coal miner continued spreading ashes in front of him, leading him gradually back to the road.

The cheers went up as the young men got back on track and turned around to thank the old gentleman, but...no one was there! There was no coal miner, no vehicle, no bucket of ashes, and no footprints in the snow to indicate that anyone had been there—not a trace—nor were there any work crew trucks or any other ashes on the road. John knew it had to have been an angel of the Lord who took care of them that day and brought them home safely without any other incident.

I dedicate this story to John's sister, Ruth Hodge Patton, who shared this testimony right before she passed into glory in October of 2018. John has since gone on to be with the Lord as well, but I surely hope that he got to meet the angel who scattered ashes around his tires on that treacherous winter's day. This is a wonderful example of how God commands His angels to watch over His children. He promises that He sends His angel ahead of us to guard us along our way.

CHAPTER 21

The Unexplained

He performs wonders that cannot be fathomed,
miracles that cannot be counted.

—Job 5:9 (NIV)

The Bible is chock-full of accounts of wonders and miracles performed by our Father who has no limits or boundaries. That same God still does the outrageous today. He has not changed nor has He lost His power but still performs the miraculous in order to display His glory and to benefit His children.

Below are some modern-day narratives of events that others have shared with me over the years that are nothing less than phenomenal!

God's Glue

Carlinda (Charli) Bergstrom

Grandma's sugar bowl after the "healing"

The windmill-shaped sugar bowl was displayed proudly on the kitchen counter like a prized trophy. Carlinda (Charli) Bergstrom had inherited it from her grandmother many years earlier upon the old woman's death. Though it meant nothing to anyone else, the cherished relic was of great sentimental value to Charli.

As a child visiting her grandparents' home in Texas, Charli remembered gazing at the little ceramic sugar-bowl house with its blue roof lid and delicate hand-painted design around its perimeter, proudly positioned at the center of the age-worn kitchen table. It held great significance to Grandma as her son had brought it home from Japan after WWII; and since Grandma had treasured it, so did Charli. Now many years later, it represented sweet memories of the summer days spent at Grandma's house and the home-cooked meals shared around that table.

One evening, as Charli and her husband Richard were entertaining some family members, one of the children dropped and broke the lid of the beloved sugar bowl into two pieces. Charli's heart sank as the tears and memories of her grandma welled up. Upon inspection, it proved to be a clean break, giving her hope that she could perhaps glue it back together to where it wouldn't look too badly deformed. But on second thought, she was afraid it might look worse and, therefore, decided to just shelve it in her office, sequestered from other curious little hands.

The fractured sugar bowl occupied the back office, out of sight and out of mind, until one particular day when Charli needed to reorganize some books on that same shelf. She picked up the sugar bowl once again to see what could be done, but to her great wonderment, the damaged lid was completely restored! Not only was it back together, but there was no seam to indicate where it could have been glued. She pulled and twisted it, trying to separate the roof pieces, but to no avail. It was most decidedly in one piece!

She rushed out of the room to query Richard. Had he glued it back together, and if so, where was the crack line? He replied in the negative. He had no idea what had happened. The only conjecture left was that the Lord had miraculously "healed" Grandma's sugar bowl! There was just no other explanation.

Knowing how much that little remembrance meant to Charli, our compassionate God restored it. He is a restorer of broken hearts, broken lives and, yes, even broken sugar bowls when they signify something important to us. In The Message in Deuteronomy 30:3, it says, "...obey him with your whole heart and soul according to everything that I command you today, God, your God, will restore everything you lost; he'll have compassion on you." There is nothing He can't do!

A Modern Translation

Louis and Millie Montecalvo

In the Book of Acts, Chapter 9, we see a story of an evangelist named Philip. The Word says that Philip found himself "caught away" by the Spirit of God. He was in one place outside of Jerusalem and then miraculously transported to Azotus (Ashdod), miles away in a split second of time.

In the 1950s, my Uncle Louis Montecalvo (whom I mentioned in an earlier chapter) had a similar experience. Uncle Lou and Aunt Millie had recently moved to Merritt Island, Florida, to pastor a church there.

One evening, they visited some members of the church, and the time went swiftly by as they enjoyed the fellowship. The hour was late when they said their good-byes and headed in the direction that they thought was home. However, being new to the area, they were unable to get their bearings and subsequently lost their way. The fact that it was a rural area with backroad orange groves and nonexistent street lights completely disoriented them. My uncle and aunt had no idea where they were and finally pulled to the side of the desolate country road they found themselves on.

Having great faith in the fact that God is a very present help in time of trouble, they asked the Holy Spirit for direction. Little did they know they were about to witness an incredible miracle. They held hands in agreement and petitioned the Lord's aid. After their amens, Uncle went to turn the key in the ignition to leave, but to their utter amazement, they found themselves sitting in their own driveway! They had been caught away just as Philip had been, supernaturally translated from one location to another.

This story is a great reminder that when we are in need, we can go to our Father to do the impossible. His hands are still performing the miraculous. Jesus said in Luke 18:27 (NIV), "What is impossible with man is possible with God." And that includes translating us if need be!

Back from the Dead

Aloah Volner

Aloah Volner was a woman with unshakeable faith. There were many times that she received healings in her body simply because she had a childlike faith that believed that "all things are possible."

On a Wednesday night some years ago, I was the guest speaker at a seniors' ministry group. Aloah and her husband, Bill, rarely missed a service. Upon finishing my message, I began to call out some healings under the anointing of the Holy Spirit. The word of knowledge came forth that someone there was having problems with a knee and was facing a knee replacement surgery. Aloah stood up to acknowledge the word. I laid hands on her swollen knee and prayed the prayer of faith and then charged her to walk in the name of Jesus. She jumped up and took a step, then another and another, and walked up and down the aisle without the aid of her cane, pain free. She declared that she was healed.

The next day, however, the pain in her knee returned, but her faith would not be moved. She reminded the devil that she had been healed the night before and commanded him to leave with his lying symptoms. With every step, she professed her healing in Jesus's name, praising God for it.

The following morning, she again experienced pain in her knee, but rather than giving up, she continued to proclaim that she was healed and to call things which were not as though they were (Romans 4:17). Aloah would not be denied.

On the morning of the third day, Aloah received her healing miracle. She awoke with no pain in her knee! She was able to walk normally without any type of aid, completely healed by the power of the Lord Jesus Christ. And no, she never did need that knee replacement surgery!

Aloah understood Hebrews 4:14, that we are to "hold firmly to the faith we profess" (confess). In Don Gossett's and E. W. Kenyon's classic book, *The Power of Your Words*, it is stated, "Faith's confession is always a joyful confession. It confesses that we have the money before it has arrived. It confesses perfect healing while pain is still in the body. It confesses victory while defeat still holds it captive."[7] Aloah held fast to the promises of God in faith, believing that it had already been done and her faith was rewarded.

Many times, I've seen people give up when their prayers were not immediately answered, but we are to hold on and keep declaring the Word of God until we see that for which we are believing. We are to envision it in our mind as if it were already answered, declare it with our mouth, and don't give up until we see it with our natural eyes. It is also important to find a scripture that speaks to our circumstance and pray it back to the Father. He is obligated to His Word for His promises are backed by the honor of His name.

Two years later, Aloah's faith would be tested again, only this time, it would be a matter of life and death.

Thursdays were choir practice nights. Bill and Aloah were faithful members of the sanctuary choir. Aloah wasn't feeling well on this particular Thursday evening but decided to attended choir practice anyway. Maybe she would feel better as the evening wore on. But that wasn't the case. Halfway through the rehearsal, Aloha lost consciousness and plummeted to the floor. I too was a member of the choir at the time, and several of us gathered around her, feverishly praying. I could see that something was drastically wrong. She wasn't stirring

---

[7] Don Gossett and E. W. Kenyon, *The Power of Your Words,* (New Kensington, PA: Whitaker House), p. 55

at all, and her eyes were rolled to the back of her head. I got down on the floor and began to speak life over her in the name of Jesus. She aroused, and we helped her back up on her chair. All color had drained from her face, and she seemed confused, mumbling things that we could not understand.

I stayed next to her, praying that strength would return to her body and that her mind would clear. A couple of minutes later, however, she lost consciousness again and slipped back on to the floor with eyes rolled back. I got back down beside her and continued to speak life over her. Once again, she rallied, and we helped her onto her chair. This time, her skin was cold. I feared the worst.

This happened three times. I knew we were warring against the spirit of death—battling for her very life. For the third time, I rebuked the spirit of death and commanded her spirit to return to her body in the name of Jesus. She let out a moan and began to move once more. I continued to speak life over her.

Someone had called an ambulance, and at that point, the paramedics arrived and took over the situation. At Bill's request, I followed the ambulance to the emergency room and sat with him until she was settled in her own room. The next morning, I called Bill to find out what had happened through the night and was startled by what he told me. He said she was doing well and would be released in a couple of days, but it was what he relayed concerning the doctor's report that was most exciting. Several tests that had been run on her heart revealed that it had stopped three times. The doctor couldn't figure out how it had kept restarting without any medical equipment or CPR being administered. Upon questioning a cardiologist, I am told that it is not possible in the natural realm for the heart to reboot on its own. It might have been a mystery to them, but not to us! We knew it was the power of the Holy Spirit that had raised her from the dead!

Two years after that incident, God did take Aloah on to her heavenly home for all eternity. Some would ask if it had been her appointed time to die on that Thursday night (Hebrews 9:27) or if God had changed His mind. I don't know. Only He knows those things, but I do know this: He will answer the prayers and petitions of the righteous for they avail much.

There are ten recorded accounts throughout the Bible of those raised from the dead, not counting the many that were resurrected at the moment of Jesus's death. (See Matthew 27:52.)

Today, there are hundreds of accounts of resurrections that have occurred all across the globe, and, as we get closer to the return of Jesus Christ, we will see more and more of these kinds of supernatural events. They will be prevalent in the last days revival, performed by those in the Body of Christ who believe.

Jesus gave this charge in Matthew 10:8 (NIV), "Heal the sick, raise the dead, cleanse those who have leprosy, drive out demons." These types of miracles are not just for those called to public ministry. We are *all* invited by the Holy Spirit to do these things. The Father has enlisted all who belong to Him to go out to the highways and byways and do the same things that He did when He walked the earth, and we are promised that, as believers, the miraculous will follow us as well.

Making a Way Where There Is No Way

Ken Freno

My brother, Ken, is four years my senior. While growing up, we called him the "fair-haired boy." It was apparent that the favor of God was on him. He had classic Italian good looks, was an outstanding scholar, and a gifted athlete. Whatever sport was in season, Ken was a participant and had the talent to back it up. But he particularly excelled in football and, in his junior year in high school, his coach set out to secure a football scholarship for him, with West Point topping off the list.

Our parents were so proud and very much relieved at the idea of a scholarship due to their own lack of resources to pay for his schooling. Unbeknownst to the rest of the family, however, Ken really didn't want to go to school on a football scholarship. He just wanted to concentrate on his studies but was aware of the fact that our parents didn't have the wherewithal to pay for his education on their own, so he acquiesced and concealed his secret from the rest of us.

Then, in the middle of that year of high school, something happened that blew the entire plan apart. Ken contracted rheumatic fever and, as a result, sustained heart damage. There was no way he could play football with a heart murmur. Now all hope was dashed of any forthcoming scholarship.

Ken deserved to go on to higher education. He had been inducted into the National Honor Society and had a real ability for math and science. He had even received some other academic scholarship funding; however, not enough that would take him through four years of a university. What were my folks to do now? Well, they did what they always did, they took it to prayer. The Word of God says, "Now the just shall live by faith..." (Hebrews 10:38, KJV). That's what our parents lived by, and God was ready to hatch a plan that none of us could have ever foreseen.

A woman in our church heard about a grant program offered by the State of Pennsylvania for students with disabilities and shared the information with my folks. Maybe Ken would qualify. Dad and Mom followed up on the tip and went to work filling out mountains of forms. They endured a series of intense interviews, and Ken had to go through several medical examinations. Then they waited...and waited; and finally, a letter arrived in the mail. Ken certainly did qualify for the subsidy and would receive a full four-year education at the state school of his choice, compliments of the State of Pennsylvania! Not only would all of his tuition be covered but so would all of his books, his school supplies, and even his medications. Ken was thrilled that he wouldn't have to play football, and our parents were overjoyed in that his schooling was covered, yet it was bittersweet in that there was still the health issue that he would have to deal with throughout his lifetime.

But the story doesn't end there. Periodically, the grant necessitated that Ken's heart be checked throughout his college years by the state. Yes, the heart murmur was still there, but strangely, he never experienced any pain, arrhythmia, shortness of breath, or discomfort of any kind. If it hadn't shown up in his physicals, it wouldn't have been apparent that he even had a problem. That was a real blessing in itself. But God still wasn't finished. After Ken graduated, he continued to have routine physical checkups and was advised that heart surgery would probably be required before his fortieth birthday. That never happened. Long before his fortieth, the heart malady just disappeared! He was mysteriously, completely healed, and it has never returned. The heart murmur had just served its purpose, and then the Lord was done with it.

Our family is convinced that the Lord utilized that heart murmur as a vehicle to provide the means to fund Ken's schooling, and when it was completed, as God's coup de grâce, He completely healed him! We can unequivocally state, as Joseph did in Genesis 50:20, that that which was meant for evil, God intended for good.

CHAPTER 22

Miraculous Healings

Fear not, my people; be glad now and rejoice,
for He has done amazing things for you.

—Joel 2:21 (TLB)

Throughout the Bible, we see many references to healing—healing of the body, mind, and spirit. Healing was part of the finished work of Calvary when Jesus broke every bondage placed on this world. Jesus came to destroy the works of the devil (1 John 3:8), including sickness and disease.

We continue to see the manifest work of the shed blood of Jesus Christ in modern-day healings. The following stories are some miraculous accounts of people who have received healings with no other explanation other than the supernatural touch of God's hand. The first account is a very real miracle that my mother experienced.

Miracles Happen

Mary Freno

SADDLEBACK MRI CENTER
23961 Calle de la Magdalena, Suite 243
Laguna Hills, CA 92653
(714) 452-3977

PATIENT: FRENO, MARY C.   DOB: 03/01/24
PHYSICIAN: ̶̶̶̶̶̶̶̶̶̶̶̶̶̶̶̶̶   RECORD # 85490

.MRI BRAIN, WITHOUT AND WITH CONTRAST   EXAM DATE: 06/11/98

CLINICAL HISTORY: Patient's previous MRI of 5-12-97 demonstrated
evidence of a right subfrontal mass which was subsequently diagnosed
at surgery as a squamous cell carcinoma. Recent endoscopic
evaluation of the nasal cavity revealed no evidence of tumor.

TECHNIQUE: MRI scanning of the brain was performed utilizing the
Siemens Magnetom system. The sequence programs used are as follows:

1. Sagittal T1-weighted images.
2. Axial T2-weighted images.
3. Axial T1-weighted images following intravenous Omniscan.
4. Coronal T1-weighted images following intravenous Omniscan.

FINDINGS: A zone of bright signal on second echo T2 imaging is seen
in the right frontal region with a small zone of similar signal to
the left of the falx cerebri in the left frontal tip. This area
shows no sign of enhancing mass effect after contrast. Its
appearance is most likely post-operative post-tumoral residual edema.
There is slight contraction of the right frontal tip compared to the
left in the region of the previous tumor. No distinct mass effect
such as displacement or distortion of normal structures is apparent.
No obvious mass effect is seen within the sinus regions or orbital
areas. The extensive pattern of right frontal vasogenic edema
previously seen has prominently diminished.

The preoperative study noted no distinct evidence of atrophy. The
current study shows aging changes which were effaced by the mass
,effect and edema. Noted is moderate prominence of ventricles, sulci
and fissures. There are a few small bright foci in cerebral white
matter indicative of subcortical arteriosclerotic microangiopathy.
There is also mild periventricular transudation. The cerebellum and
the brain stem remain normal.

(CONTINUED)

Saddleback MRI Medical Group   23961 Calle de la Magdalena, Suite 243
                                Laguna Hills, CA 92653   (714) 452-3977

The medical report after my mother's healing

I stepped out of the doctor's office, leaving my parents to finish up the appointment, grateful that I had another meeting to attend and could escape from that room. I shut the door behind me and, seeing a private alcove nearby, ducked inside to hide myself, giving way to the sob stifled in my throat and the hot tears that had collected at the brim of my eyes.

I had accompanied my mom and dad to the doctor's office to receive the results of an MRI scan of my mother's head. The prognosis not only shocked but absolutely devastated me.

"You have a malignant tumor that has extended into the brain," the doctor told my mother. "It is too widespread and is therefore inoperable. I'm so sorry to tell you, but there is really nothing we can do for you. You probably have about six to eight weeks to live."

The tumor had originated in her nasal cavity and had spread into the frontal lobe of her skull, breaking through the brain barrier. There was also a large mass behind her right eye.

We tried three other doctors, but the same diagnosis was confirmed by them all.

In April of 1997, Mom thought she had the flu. Her sense of smell had disappeared, and she noticed that she would lean to the right when she walked. The week of Mother's Day, while sitting at the breakfast table, she blacked out and fell unconscious to the floor. After a call to 911 and an ambulance ride to the emergency room, tests were finally run that gave us the answer we didn't want to hear. From that point on, Mom's health quickly deteriorated, and she was confined to her bed or a wheelchair.

Regardless of what all the doctors were declaring, my mother had a steadfast faith. In the early days of her diagnosis, she stated very matter-of-factly that "this isn't going to get me down." And she meant it. She never complained or cried out, "Why me?" She truly trusted God with her life, and it spoke volumes to those of us around her. Her faith boosted our faith!

My dad would not allow any of us to speak anything negative about her condition nor would he even remotely discuss any kind of funeral plans or burial plots. Oft times, he would lay his Bible on Mom's head and pray the Word of God over her. Other times, he would put the Bible on the floor and stand on it, signifying that he was standing on the Word and would quote healing scriptures. We were all at the crossroads between believing the Word that we had preached all those years or not.

One night, as I was diligently praying for Mom, I clearly heard the Lord say, "Raise up an army to pray for your mother." In obedience to His instructions, my family and I called upon all of our friends, relatives, our churches, and every ministry we knew to put her on their prayer lists. Within days, thousands of people were praying on her behalf.

As the weeks pressed on with no improvement in sight, the family felt that we needed to at least try some kind of treatment and be proactive in spite of being told that no treatment would work.

First, she was given chemotherapy but violently reacted to it after only three treatments and was rushed back to the hospital. She hit her lowest point that night, and we really thought the Lord was going to take her home. I called our pastor, Darrell Ward, and he and his wife, Lenora, came and prayed over her. Pastor Darrell began to speak life into her body in Jesus's name, and it was as if electricity filled the room.

When I returned to the hospital the next morning, I was astonished to see my mom sitting up in an easy chair with all of her intravenous tubes removed and her mind clear! Though she was not completely healed, we recognized that God was definitely in the mix.

This gave us new hope, and we pushed on. Next, we researched radiation treatments. At the time, the protocol was to radiate the entire head, and though a few doctors did suggest we try it, we were cautioned that she would probably lose the sight in her right eye and possibly both eyes. We decided to put it off and kept searching for an alternative. From a medical standpoint, there was no good news no matter where we turned, but our hope was not in the medical reports, our hope was in the report of the Lord.

The weeks turned into months, and Mom passed the two-month medical death sentence. We were encouraged. Summer came and went, and she was still with us, but during that time, we hit another crisis. A lump appeared on her nose next to her right eye, indicating that the cancer had continued to spread. Again, we were faced with the only treatment option left—radiation.

However, God was still working. I had heard about a new radiation treatment called the peacock. That protocol used a light beam that targeted only the cancerous tumor, leaving the surrounding area untouched which, in her case, would mean her eyes. Today, it is standard treatment, but at that time, it was in its early stages, and there were only seven hospitals in the country that offered this type of radiation. I made several phone calls, praying that I could find one close enough to us. As the Lord would have it, UC Irvine Medical Center was one of the seven, which was only twenty miles away. I was ecstatic! There are no "happenstances" in God's plans for our lives.

The doctor in charge of the program said she would take Mom on; however, she candidly stated that because of the enormity of the mass, we could only expect the radiation to somewhat shrink the tumor but not completely eradicate it. It would perhaps extend her life some additional months. That was all she could offer. We were willing to take the chance and trusted God with the rest.

After thirty-three treatments, there was nothing else that could be done for her. A month after the treatments were complete, an MRI showed that only 30 percent of the tumor had shrunk. We were disappointed that it hadn't diminished beyond that, but were told to give the radiation another month to work. Perhaps it would decrease in size a little more.

On May 5, 1998, one year to the date of her cancer diagnosis, Mom had an appointment with her ears, nose and throat specialist. That morning, she awoke with a song running through her spirit, "I Am the God That Healeth Thee." She wondered if the Lord was trying to tell her something and went to her appointment with great anticipation.

The doctor did a biopsy. He was stunned! All tests were negative. That couldn't be! He sent her to have another MRI, and it was confirmed—there was no tumor, no cancer! But beyond that, there wasn't even any scar tissue to indicate that there had ever been a tumor there! All of her doctors admitted that it was a miracle. There was nothing medically they could point to that would explain her cure. In the natural realm, it made no sense.

The tumor never returned for the Father sealed the deal. Like Hezekiah, my mom was granted fifteen more years and lived to be the ripe old age of eighty-eight before she quietly passed in her sleep from this life into the presence of the Lord

One of the names of God is Jehovah Rophe, "The Lord that Healeth Thee." Rophe in Hebrew means "to restore, to heal, or to make healthful." We find that reference in Exodus 15:26 (KJV), "For I am the Lord that healeth thee." In every way, Mom was restored, healed, and made healthful.

The Lord is the ultimate Healer, who is still doing the miraculous today. My mother's healing is just one of many supernatural healings I have seen over the years. This next testimony is shared by a lady who had a spectacular healing by way of a trip to heaven.

A Trip to Heaven

Deborah Stewart

Deborah Stewart worked as the secretary of a church and Christian school in Southern California in the late 1970s. She liked her job that included the additional responsibilities of overseeing the church ministries. Over time, however, she began to see some mishandling of finances and unseemly conduct within the ministerial ranks. Deborah thought about resigning, but because of extenuating circumstances within her family, she felt she needed to stay.

As the corruption became increasingly apparent, Deborah felt trapped and helpless. Needing wisdom and guidance, she did the only thing she knew to do—fast and pray that God would intervene in what seemed to be an impossible situation.

In the summer of 1978, Deborah became deathly ill from the despair and burden of it all. She had been fasting off and on for six months and, as a result, became anorexic. She lost more than fifty pounds and had no appetite for food whatever. When she did try to eat, her system could not keep the food down, and because of her lack of nutrition and weakened condition, Deborah's body could not fend off infections.

She continued to get weaker and weaker until, one day, she began to have chest pains and could not breathe. She crawled out of her bed and collapsed into a nearby rocking chair, hoping to gain some breath by sitting up. As she closed her eyes, gasping for her last painful gulp of air, Deborah's spirit quietly slipped out from her body and was instantly transported to heaven.

Although she was in the supernatural realm, she continued to have thought process. She was conscious of the fact that she had died and was distinctly aware of being in heaven and all that was around her. Deborah looked down to inspect her heavenly attire. She was clothed in what looked like a bright white robe and was surprised to see that she still had a woman's body. What was more, she experienced no pain nor did she have any fear. All was peaceful.

She looked around her. There was so much to take in. The beautiful surroundings overwhelmingly appealed to all of her senses. The path on which she stood was made of an iridescent gold yet so pure that it appeared to be see-through, exposing the grass beneath it. The grass was the greenest green she had ever seen, emerald in color, standing about two inches high and as thick as a carpet that seemingly stretched on forever. Everything around her was alive. Even the rarefied air could be "tasted" like a fresh rainy day. There was no sun, but everything was illuminated with a holy light, lit up by the glory of God, with the most perfect and comfortable temperature. Voices of an angelic choir filled the atmosphere singing praises to God and extolling His countless attributes. Though there were several different harmonies, it sounded like one voice. The music didn't seem to have an origin but was part of the air of heaven itself.

To Deborah's delight, immediately ahead of her was a wall displaying an abundance of giant tropical flowers, triple the size of those on earth. They were in the vein of deep purples and pinks, yet their brilliant colors were unmatched to any she had ever seen on this planet. Some of the foliage was arrayed in colors only known in heaven. On the other side of the wall stood a lone tree, displaying unusual leaves that were reminiscent of lace. Deborah did not recognize this species of tree but later discovered this same kind on earth and was able to identify it as a type of eucalyptus.

Her greatest joy, however, was that Jesus, her Savior and Lord, was there to meet her upon her arrival. He was much taller than she had expected, and His white robe blazed with the glory of God. He emanated all love, acceptance, and peace toward her, and she felt no condemnation from Him. His love was unconditional, but He did make it clear to her that He does hold His children accountable to the call on their lives, regardless of what others think, say, or do. This was very important to Him.

Jesus and Deborah continued to converse through thoughts rather than spoken words. She asked Him many questions regarding her personal life, but she had one that topped her list. Along with her secretarial position, Deborah was called to a frontline ministry. She would go out and preach, raised up by God to do a task that mostly men were called to do. Though times are changing, women who are called to the pulpit are still often rejected and opposed, and Deborah had experienced plenty of that.

"So, Lord, why did you call me to that position rather than a man?" she inquired.

The Lord was gracious to answer her. "I have allowed it to build character in you and teach you to persevere in opposition."

In Joel 2:28, it is made clear that in the last days, God will pour out His spirit upon "all flesh," which includes His daughters. He calls and equips those whom He so chooses, and obviously, in this passage of scripture, women are included. God is looking for those who will answer the call and be obedient to Him, regardless of gender, age, race, or social status.

As Deborah and the Lord walked and communed, she observed a dense forest to her right with a large stream running through it. Further up, she could see a magnificent bridge spanning the stream, covered with the same enormous flowers she had seen earlier. As they approached the bridge, Deborah knew that if she crossed over, it would be the point of no return. However, the Lord made it clear that the choice was hers to continue on or return. She had one more question, though, before she made her decision.

"Lord, if I cross over now, will I see my kids in heaven?"

The Lord candidly answered, "No," but did indicate that if she returned back to earth, she would have an impact on their lives, and they would indeed enter in.

"Then I'm going back," she answered decisively. She had to continue to minister to her family and do all that she could to bring them into the Kingdom of God. With that, her spirit immediately rejoined her body that was still slumped over the rocking chair in her bedroom, and life returned.

But this time, something was different. She felt no more pain or sickness, and she was hungry—oh so hungry! She ran to the kitchen and sat down on the floor in front of the open refrigerator door, grabbing and gobbling whatever she could find to eat. Now…would she be able to keep the food down? Yes!

Deborah was instantaneously and completely healed by the mighty hand of God, and as she puts it, she hasn't stopped eating since! She eventually left the church where she had worked and has gone on to continue her speaking ministry.

Deborah shares her story to let others know that heaven is a real place, and that if Jesus is your Lord and Savior, you have nothing to fear but will only have gain. Earthly words cannot accurately describe what awaits us there. The Apostle Paul states in 1 Corinthians 2:9 (NIV), "No eye has seen, no ear has heard, no mind has conceived what God has prepared for those who love him."

The Breath of God

Leslie Hurtado

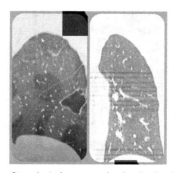

The MRI of Leslie's lung with the hole (left photo)

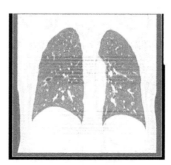

The MRI of Leslie's lung after her healing (left photo)

Leslie Hurtado was understandably concerned when her recent CT scan revealed a three-centimeter (1.18 inch) hole in her right lung. Whether it was attributed to the aspiration pneumonia she had recently battled or a growing cancer, the doctors as yet could not say, but breathing was getting more and more difficult. Besides this disconcerting diagnosis, she was already scheduled for a badly needed surgery to correct a severe hiatal hernia.

Two weeks later, as Leslie was recuperating at home from the hernia procedure, someone knocked on her front door. Her thirteen-year-old son, Shawn, answered and was met by an estranged ex-boyfriend of Leslie's. Their relationship had not ended well, and he was incensed by the rejection. He pushed his way into the house and violently assaulted Shawn with a blow to his face that left him with a black eye. Leslie's eleven-year-old daughter, Alexis, screamed as she witnessed the heinous deed, and her scream caused Leslie to rush from her bedroom to the front of the house. There, she came face-to-face with her worst nightmare. Her assailant grabbed her and brutally hurled her across the room. Satisfied with the harm he had intended to inflict, he stormed out of the house.

Leslie had traversed the tile floor face down and slammed into a sofa, which left her not only with multiple contusions but with excruciating chest pains and breathing difficulties. Thinking perhaps there was further damage to the opening in her lung, she drove herself to a local emergency room. Upon examination by the ER doctor, she was advised to contact her surgeon straightaway. The surgeon ran several tests and noted that there was no further injury to the hole in her lung but that the impact of the attack had ruptured her esophagus and pushed it through the fresh incision. This caused the esophagus to rest on her heart thus creating the chest pain. It was a very dangerous state of affairs, and another immediate surgery was necessitated.

On September 5, 2017, Leslie was wheeled back into the operating room, a day that would forever change her life. Her doctor, realizing the severity of the damage that had been done, was apprehensive about the surgery and tried to prepare her for the grim news that she was facing a life-and-death situation. Not only was the damage severe, but since she had just had the hiatal surgery two weeks before, revisiting that same area could also prove extremely dangerous. Regardless of the treacherous condition she was in, however, there were no other options. She had to have that operation.

Leslie's life hung in the balance as the length of the surgery dragged on. In the midst of the struggle to fix the tangled mess of her insides, what her doctor feared the most came to pass. Leslie went into cardiac arrest...twice. The surgical team worked feverishly to resuscitate her, and after several intense minutes, they were finally able to stabilize her heart and finish up the surgery.

Though quite weak, Leslie did make it through, but she was plagued by the memory of a strange and very vivid dream she had while undergoing surgery. Or was it a dream? It seemed so real and was extremely frightening.

A few days later, her doctor disclosed that she had literally died twice on the operating table, and it was then she realized that what she had experienced had not been a dream at all but was the reality of her soul departing her body on its way to a dark hopeless eternity. At the time of her death, her surroundings went completely dark, and four very black malevolent creatures appeared, ready to transport her into hell. Each had two large black wings that wrapped around her body, throwing her into the greatest terror she had ever known. As they began to overtake her spirit to carry her to her eternal damnation, the Lord Jesus appeared, along with Leslie's maternal grandparents, who had passed on some years before. She hadn't known them well, but her mom told her that they "prayed a lot."

The light of Jesus's glory dispelled the inky darkness, and although Leslie could not distinguish the Lord's facial features, she could see that He had brown shoulder-length hair and wore a white shimmering robe-like garment.

The Lord boomed out at the satanic inhabitants of hell, "Oh, no you don't! She still has work to do."

At that, the creatures instantly released their hold and quickly vanished into the ground.

The Lord Jesus then addressed Leslie. In contrast to the way He spoke to the demons, His voice toward her was calm, soothing, and reassuring. "I am fighting for you. You have two babies who need you, but you must promise me that you will write this story, as it will change lives for my glory."

Leslie left the hospital a couple of weeks later with a new resolve and zeal for life. Prior to her time in the hospital, she had been depressed and wanted to end it all, but now, having encountered the living God, she was determined to carry out the promise she had made to Him. The first thing she knew she had to do was get her life right with her Maker. She contacted Pastor JJ (Jerry) Borja, the pastor of the First Assembly of God Church in Adelanto, California, who invited her to come to service that coming Sunday morning. There, she and her two children prayed the sinner's prayer and dedicated their lives to follow the One True Messiah.

There was still the matter of her health, however. Until the esophagus wound could heal, she continuously had to carry a nutrition bag on her back that contained enriched liquid that fed her body through a tube. The bigger issue, though, was the hole in her lung and the oxygen tank that she had to tote wherever she went to help her breathe. Worse yet, the gaping crater now caused her extreme pain with every breath she took. Her lung surgeon chose not to operate at the time since she had already had so many surgeries but preferred to watch to see if the hole became any larger. His major concern was that if the hole continued to grow, it would be necessary to remove half the lung.

This was the situation Leslie was in when I met her at the Adelanto church one Sunday morning not long after her surgery. Pastor JJ introduced us and asked if I would pray for her healing. During prayer time, Leslie approached the altar area assisted by her daughter. I could see she was in a great deal of pain. I asked her a couple of questions regarding her health and tried to build some faith in her to believe for the supernatural hand of God to heal her.

My prayer team and I proceeded to lay hands on her, rebuking the pain and commanding the lung aperture to close up in the mighty name of Jesus. I then told her to take a step of faith by taking the breathing apparatus out of her nose and breathe in the Holy Spirit-saturated air that surrounded us. By faith, Leslie complied and took a deep breath. She took another and another. All discomfort was gone! Joyful tears soaked her pain-worn face as she came to the realization that she was instantaneously healed by the miraculous hand of God.

She grabbed her daughter and cried out, "Baby, it doesn't hurt!"

I said to her, "Say that again!"

She repeated it again. "It doesn't hurt to breathe!"

The whole church burst out in praise! Dr. Jesus had shown up in power!

Leslie went to her doctor not long afterward and had him do another CT scan. The hollow space in her lung wall had completely closed. The only evidence that there had actually been something unseemly there was a remnant of scar tissue. The doctor was baffled. Leslie says, "He still scratches his head as to how it closed. He says it's a medical mystery." A medical mystery? Probably. A divine mystery? No! We know that Leslie was made whole by the wondrous work of our Lord Jesus's hands!

"Praise the Lord, O my soul, and forget not all his benefits— who forgives all your sins and heals all your diseases, who redeems your life from the pit and crowns you with love and compassion" Psalm 103:2–4 (NIV).

Death Travels in Threes

Bishop Dexter Kilpatrick

The bishop's car after the accident

Bishop Dexter Kilpatrick, Senior Pastor of Spirit of Christ Tabernacle in Victorville, California, felt uneasy that morning in 2005 before driving down Reche Canyon Road in Colton, California. Having known the voice of God since he was a child, he sensed that God was giving him a warning. He wasn't sure what it meant, but the feeling was so strong that he contacted his godson in hopes that he would come to his location and drive him to his appointments. Unfortunately, his godson was unable to accommodate him, and there was nothing else to do but ask for Divine protection and start driving.

Bishop Kilpatrick's mission that day was to meet another pastor to set up a new ministry in San Bernardino, California. With no other options available, he began his journey, trusting God to take care of him. To calm his mind, the bishop sang praises and worshipped the Lord, all the while keeping his focus on the winding mountain pass before him. He was well aware of Reche Canyon Road's reputation for many horrific accidents, and all of his senses were on alert as he negotiated the twists and turns.

Upon reaching the flat valley, he gave a sigh of relief, assuming that the worst of the drive was behind him. However, as he steered his car around a bend, a utility truck being driven by a drunk driver crossed into the pastor's lane and struck him head on. Not only was the front-end demolished, but the weight and momentum of the impact pushed the utility truck on to the roof of the car, where it came to rest.

A third driver in a pickup truck saw the wreck ahead but was unable to stop before plunging into the right side of the bishop's automobile, crushing the passenger door. With both doors now compacted and the roof compressed, Bishop Kilpatrick was completely pinned inside.

The drivers of the trucks were unharmed and ran to try to pry the car doors open to rescue the bishop but to no avail. The call went out to 911, and the first responders arrived, but no one was able to force the doors open.

Meanwhile, inside the car, the airbags had deployed, knocking the bishop unconscious for a short period of time. When he came to, he was staring at the front bumper of his own car which had rammed through the windshield. He took assessment of his surroundings and observed the chaos of those who were trying to help outside and knew his situation was dire. Fear began to mount, and in the midst of the horror, he heard the taunting voice of the evil one in his inner man say, "Sing your songs of Zion now."

Satan, the enemy of both God and man, throws out lies and disparaging words in the hope that we will pick them up and agree with them. Once we agree, he then has us. We will begin to think things contrary to the Word of God. It is imperative that we are in the Word and understand what it says or we will be swayed into thinking thoughts that are not of God. We need to rebuff those destructive thoughts and replace them with the promises in the Bible. Scripture says in 2 Corinthians 10:5 (KJV) that we are to cast down "imaginations, and every high thing that exalteth itself against the knowledge of God, and bring into captivity every thought to the obedience of Christ." We are to align ourselves with His Word no matter how bad conditions may look in the natural. We speak what God speaks and need to see what God sees.

Though the situation looked next to impossible, Bishop Kilpatrick was not to be bamboozled by the Great Deceiver. His faith was in the Lord and he cried out, "Jesus, I need you now!" As he said these words, he noticed a tiny gap in the bumper-filled windshield that gave visibility to the sky. Through it, he caught sight of an angel descending a ladder like a heavenly fireman coming to his rescue. The angel turned around to look at him as if to say, "I'm coming to help you."

But things went from bad to worse. The tottering truck perched on the roof listed and then crashed further into the interior of the car and hurled the dashboard down onto the bishop's legs. Kilpatrick screamed out in pain. The blow caused his left leg to break in seven places, which included the fibula, femur, and the tibia, with bone poking through the flesh. Additionally, it shredded the main artery that leads from the leg to the heart. He was told later that that alone should have killed him.

The pain was excruciating. "God, why is the angel taking so long?" he bemoaned. "Help me!" At that moment, there was a loud bang, and the car shook as if there had been an earthquake. At first, he thought another car had hit him, but that was not the case. To his amazement, the shaking caused the passenger door to fling open— on its own. The jolt also caused the bishop's leg to be dislodged from under the dashboard and bend upward, seemingly by its own effort! He felt his body shift as if someone was turning him. And then, incredibly, he was lifted up by the angel, floated out of the mangled car, and was gently deposited onto the curb. Though he could see the angel in action, the crowd that had congregated outside the car could not; they could only see the bishop gliding out and settling on the curb. Stunned and speechless, they stepped back and watched as the scene played out. What in the world had they just witnessed?

The bishop avowed that if he was going to die, he was going to go out preaching, and he took the opportunity to piggyback on the phenomenon by telling the throng about the miracle-working Jesus. It touched the hearts of all the people there, including the paramedics, and many tears were shed upon hearing the Gospel message. No one could believe that he was still alive let alone supernaturally rescued! By all accounts, he should have expired.

The first responders wheeled him into the ambulance and told him that he would be taken to Loma Linda University Medical Center, but again he sensed the same foreboding that he had felt earlier that day. He argued with the paramedics not to take him to Loma Linda; however, it was the closest hospital and so, against his better judgment, he agreed.

Upon their arrival at the medical campus, he was carried out of the ambulance and immediately recognized that his apprehension was for good reason. Looking up, he spied three ominous-looking black vultures circling the pinnacle of the hospital.

"God, why are they here?" The answer he received was rather daunting.

"They are here for you. Death travels in threes." But before he could react to what had he had just heard, a nurse came through the doors of the ER.

As she passed by him, she touched his shoulder and simply stated, "All is well," and moved on. His peace returned—peace that he would need for the news he would receive from the surgeon inside.

Because of the extensive damage to his left leg, there was no way of saving it. The doctor delivered the sad news that his leg would have to be amputated up to the hip. At that, he told the surgeon that he wanted to pray for the operating team before they proceeded, and as he did, the glory of heaven manifested again, and the surgeon and entire team were in tears, touched by the One Who Sits on Heaven's Throne. The bishop was then transported into the operating room. He was now completely in the hands of Almighty God.

And *that* was the best place to be, for when Bishop Kilpatrick regained consciousness in recovery, he felt for the gap in his body where his leg would have been, but there was no gap. His leg was intact! The surgeon did not have to amputate it after all. He was able to operate on the leg and perform a procedure that restored it. As Bishop Kilpatrick puts it, "God used his (the surgeon's) hands to do what was not medically achievable." Another miracle had taken place.

But his battle was not over yet. While still in recovery, he was given morphine for pain. Not knowing that a painkiller had already been administered, a different nurse gave him a dose of another high-potency narcotic. This caused him to overdose, lose consciousness, and flat line. Death came knocking, and immediately, his spirit left his body.

As he transitioned into the heavenly realm, his whole life played out before him, both the good and the bad, as if on a movie screen. He was then immediately ushered into the presence of God, where he experienced only peace and tranquility. There were no tears nor did he feel any pain or fear. Though all was perfect and glorious, he did not want to stay because he knew his youngest daughter still needed him back on earth; and so, after earnestly requesting the Father that he be permitted to live, he slipped back into his body and returned to this world.

Having been graciously granted a second chance at life, he and his wife, Brigitte, are now ministering together as a dynamic duo for the Kingdom of Heaven. Bishop Dexter Kilpatrick has no fear of dying when the time comes for the Lord to take him home for good. He knows firsthand what Paul meant when he wrote in Philippians 1:21 (NIV), "For to me, to live is Christ and to die is gain."

God's hand is at work in our lives constantly. Sometimes we aren't aware of it, and at other times, He makes a big splash, as in the testimonies above, but He's always there—honing, shaping, rescuing, providing, protecting, healing, delivering, and saving. And He has called each of us to be a reflection of those things before the world so that His glory will be made known and so that many will come to the knowledge of Jesus Christ.

I believe that these stories are downpayments of what is to come. These types of events are signposts of what more we can expect and a foreshadowing of the miracles that are poised to happen soon in the coming end time revival. God's glory will be very evident through obvious miracles that He is going to flood the earth with in order to draw millions, yea, even billions, of souls into the Kingdom before His return. Therefore, I submit to you that we must ready ourselves for the last days harvest by discovering the gifts that God has equipped us with and begin to operate in those gifts so that we are ready to take the place that God has designed for each one of us.

EPILOGUE

One very ordinary Sunday morning, several years ago, while worshipping in my home church, the Lord opened my eyes into the spirit realm, a "suddenly" moment when everything in my world faded and an overlay of the spiritual dimension took front and center.

I saw hundreds of horses confined in a regular corral. They were of various breeds, colors, and sizes. The horses were restless, prancing and bumping against one another. Some whinnied and some reared up on their hind legs, all anxious to be released from their confinement to open spaces.

Then I saw an angel of the Lord come and unlock the gate, releasing the horses and allowing them to race from their pen into a myriad of directions across the earth. They all seemed to have a particular destination and purpose, innately knowing their own direction.

I questioned the Lord as to what this could mean. He answered immediately and said, "These are the ones I have been preparing for the last days revival. They are restless to go out and fulfill my calling on their lives, but their time is not yet. However, at the appointed time, I will release them to go out into their designated sphere of influence and do My will, sharing the Good News of Jesus Christ with signs and wonders following. This will be the last spiritual outpouring before my return."

Perhaps this resonates in your spirit. Perhaps you are one of those horses sitting in obscurity, knowing you have been called and have been knocking at the panels of the corral, wanting to be released into the fullness of your destiny. Or perhaps you are just beginning to set sail into your own journey. Regardless of where you are in your spiritual trek, I urge you, my destined friends, to not be weary in your well-doing and faint not at the continual work you do for God's Kingdom. In due season, you will reap a harvest if you are faithful to the task He has given you, and at the exact appointed time, the Lord will open the gate to release you into you all He has predestined you to do. May He use you exceedingly abundantly above all you could ever ask or think for you are the work of His hands.

KEEP IN TOUCH

IT'S BEGINNING TO RAIN MINISTRIES, INC.

To book a speaking engagement, send an email to:
info@itsbeginningtorain.com

For more information on this ministry, go to:
Website: www.itsbeginningtorain.com
Facebook: http://www.facebook.com/rainministries

THE WORK OF HIS HANDS:

TARGETING YOUR SPIRITUAL GIFTS

The Work of His Hands: Targeting Your Spiritual Gifts Workbook is a must for those seeking to discover their purpose and destiny and contains the following tools to assist in the journey:

- The Personal Spiritual Gifts Assessment that will target each person's gift-mix
- The Fruit of the Spirit Self-Evaluation that will point out strengths and weaknesses in one's spiritual walk
- Worksheets that correlate to Section 2 in the main book, *The Work of His Hands: Targeting Your Spiritual Gifts*, for individual or classroom Bible study
- Guide sheets that will help connect one's spiritual gifts to his/her destiny

ABOUT THE AUTHOR

Photo by Ryan M. Brewer

Rev. Linda C. Triska, Founder and CEO of *It's Beginning to Rain Ministries, Inc.*, has been sharing the Gospel of Jesus Christ for over thirty years. Since answering the call of God in 1984, Linda has been a popular and sought-after guest speaker in churches, ministry groups, conferences, and retreats. She is known for developing and teaching the "Targeting Your Spiritual Gifts" series, motivating others to rise up in their gifts and callings.

Additionally, Pastor Linda has hosted "It's Beginning to Rain," an international Christian television talk show that aired on the Faith Unveiled Network and KVVB TV reaching into several countries throughout the world with the Gospel. The broadcast also streamed on digital platforms.

Linda has worked in the private business sector as well as having worked in entertainment as a model and actress in television, films, and commercials.

In both 2010 and 2013, Linda was honored by being named "Inspiring Woman of the Year" by the Daily Press Newspaper and Today's Woman Foundation in the California High Desert for her work in establishing Feed My Sheep in the High Desert, a food pantry feeding several thousand low-income families per year. The pantry was also named "Non-Profit of the Year" by the High Desert Resource Network in 2012.

Rev. Triska holds a Bachelor of Science degree in Business Administration with a teaching credential and is a licensed and ordained minister. She and her husband, Brad, live in Southern California and they have a married daughter.